ESSENTIAL
DENVER

Discovery and Exploration Guide

LISA J. SHULTZ

Essential Denver: Discovery and Exploration Guide
Published by High Country Publications
Denver, Colorado
Copyright © 2020 by Lisa J. Shultz. All rights reserved.
LisaJShultz.com

Publisher's Cataloging-in-Publication data

Names: Shultz, Lisa J., author.
Title: Essential Denver : discover and exploration guide. / by Lisa J. Shultz.
Description: First trade paperback original edition. | Denver [Colorado] : High
Country Publications, 2020. | Also published as an ebook.
Identifiers: ISBN 978-0-9986509-5-1
Subjects: LCSH: Travel. | Colorado—Denver.
BISAC: TRAVEL / United States / West / Mountain.
Classification: LCC F774.3 | DDC 917.88–dc22

Book Design and Cover Design © 2020
Cover and Interior Design by Victoria Wolf, wolfdesignandmarketing.com
Editing by Jennifer Jas, Words With Jas, LLC, wordswithjas.com

This book is printed in the United States of America.

CONTENTS

INTRODUCTION

I LOVE DENVER! In my midlife, I found myself reconnecting with the rich history of my hometown by taking walking tours and reading history books. I decided to share my knowledge of Denver with visitors and the many newcomers who move to the Mile High City, so I could enrich their experience and mine. Those who were born in Denver or those who have lived in the city most of their lives might also enjoy rediscovering places they have not visited in years and uncovering facts they have forgotten or perhaps never knew.

Why did I write this book? I want to make Denver's vast history and many landmarks easy to digest. My previous book *Lighter Living: Declutter. Organize. Simplify.* paved the way to this purposefully light summary. As I discerned what I thought was essential as a starting point to include in this book, I hoped my readers would be inspired to dig deeper in the areas that interest them most. After reading *Essential Denver*, you may want to visit sites, take walks and gaze upon structures and neighborhoods with a fresh perspective. If you want the detailed history, you can find several excellent Denver history books, which I list in my Recommendations section. I have read those books from cover to cover; however, many people are daunted by or avoid reading history books. I hope that readers will enjoy and remember my distilled entries of history, people and places, and feel inspired to explore further.

In most cases, I only included buildings still standing and points of interest within Denver City and County. Occasionally I branched out from city and county lines when I thought it was relevant to understanding Denver's evolution. The entries in each section are not necessarily in alphabetical order but instead may be in order of age or historical significance. I had to stop somewhere when it came to including buildings, people, neighborhoods and places of interest. Subsequent editions might expand my original lists with reader feedback and the changes in Denver over time. I hope to appeal to all generations. I have attempted, to the best of my abilities, to fact check and provide accurate information, current as of the publishing date of this edition.

How did I write this book? I took tours, read many books and researched multiple online resources. I condensed all those methods into short entries and then listed websites to learn more about each subject.

WHO THIS BOOK IS FOR:

- Tourists who want to learn about the city while visiting

- Newcomers who want to explore their new city

- Longtime residents and those born in Denver who want to rediscover history and the places they may have forgotten about, overlooked or never knew about

- People who like history in small doses

- School-aged children who desire a concise overview of Denver

- Teachers who want to use the book as a history teaching aid and to schedule outings to various locations

- Lyft, taxi and Uber drivers who want to educate and entertain their passengers

Enjoy discovering and exploring Denver!

Cheers,
Lisa J. Shultz

Follow Essential Denver on social media, where you can see more photos and updates. Share your photography using the tag #EssentialDenver.

LisaJShultz.com
facebook.com/essentialdenver
instagram.com/essentialdenver
pinterest.com/lisajaneshultz/essential-denver

DENVER FOUNDING

LET US START WITH AN OVERVIEW of the early inhabitants
and settlers of the Denver area. Before the Euro-American prospectors and settlers arrived, Native American tribes lived in the area of
Denver. The Native American Apache tribe may have been the first
people in the Denver area in the 1500s. They hunted buffalo and culti-
vated crops in and near rivers of the area. In the 1700s, the Comanche
tribe arrived and forced the Apaches south. Then the Kiowa tribe
came to the area, first fighting with the Comanches and then allying
with them. In the 1800s, Arapaho and Cheyenne tribes arrived and
drove the Ute tribe into the mountains.

The Denver area was also home to trappers and mountain men
in the 1800s. French trappers had a rendezvous with the Arapaho,
Cheyenne and Kiowa tribes in 1815 near what is now known as
Littleton. In the 1830s, Louis Vasquez established a fur trading post

at the confluence of the South Platte River and Clear Creek.

Those who live in Denver today and enjoy the many trees in the city may not realize there were originally no trees in the area except a few cottonwoods along the rivers. In 1820, Major Stephen H. Long explored eastern Colorado, including the area that would later be settled as Denver. He declared the region the "Great American Desert" and did not consider it habitable. The California Gold Rush (1848–1855) prompted a western migration of 300,000 prospectors in search of mining opportunities. The Colorado Gold Rush was a few years behind that of California.

The official founding date of Denver is November 1858. That year, several groups arrived at the confluence of Cherry Creek and the South Platte River. William Green Russell led the first prospecting party to arrive. The Russell group called their settlement Auraria (meaning gold), which lay on the southwestern side of Cherry Creek. Auraria was Russell's hometown in Georgia. A second group, led by John Easter, settled across Cherry Creek from the Russell contingent. The Easter group named their settlement St. Charles. While Easter was gone to Kansas in an attempt to get an official charter, a third group, led by General William Larimer, arrived and took over the St. Charles side, calling it Denver City. Competition between Auraria and Denver City ensued. Newcomers were enticed to both sides of the river in a bitter rivalry. Finally, in 1860, Auraria and Denver created a merger on the Larimer Street Bridge over Cherry Creek.

These first prospector groups panned for gold at the confluence of Cherry Creek and the South Platte River in 1858, but they didn't find much there. However, in January of 1859, the Colorado Gold Rush began when the first substantial gold discovery in the state was made near Idaho Springs. Denver eventually became a supply hub for the many prosperous mines in the mountains west of Denver.

DENVER NAMESAKE

James William Denver was described as a politician, soldier and lawyer. The man our city was named after never resided here, although he reportedly visited twice briefly. He was born in Winchester, Virginia, on October 23, 1817. Educated at the University of Cincinnati, he then taught school and practiced law. In 1847, he fought in the Mexican–American War. Later he moved to California. Involved in a duel, he killed newspaper editor Edward Gilbert in 1852. He soon became a California State Senator, then Secretary of State of California, and in 1854, he was elected as a US Congressman.

He became governor of Kansas Territory during 1858. He also served in the Civil War as a brigadier general. He died on August 9, 1892, in Wilmington, Ohio.

DENVER NICKNAMES

The Mile High City is Denver's most well-known nickname since it is 5,280 feet, or a mile, above sea level. On the State Capitol steps, you will find a designation for the mile-high point. Technology improvements created alterations of which step was officially chosen, so you will find more than one marker today.

Other Denver nicknames include:

- Queen City of the Plains
- Queen City of the West
- Convention City
- Wall Street of the West
- Cow Town
- Broncoville

DENVER FLAG, SEAL AND LOGO

FLAG

In 1926, Denver's flag was designed by a student of Denver North High School, Margaret Overbeck. The yellow circle in the center symbolizes the sun and gold in the Colorado mountains. The circle is centered in the flag, just as Denver is in the center of the state, and is surrounded by blue representing the sky. Below the yellow circle is a white zigzag representing Native American heritage, and the red below that represents the earth and our state's name, Colorado.

SEAL

Denver's corporate seal was designed in 1901 by Denver artist Henry Read. This round corporate seal shows an eagle, key and a capitol dome. The dome indicates Denver as the capital of Colorado.

The key represents Denver as the entry to the Rocky Mountains and the eagle reminds us that Denver is a free American city.

LOGO

Denver's logo has an image of the letter "D" with the word Denver to the right of it and The Mile High City below the word Denver.

FURTHER EXPLORATION

Flag

en.wikipedia.org/wiki/Flag_of_Denver

Seal

denvergov.org/content/denvergov/en/denver-marketing-and-media-services/brand-guidelines/logo-seal.html

Logo

denvergov.org/content/denvergov/en/denver-marketing-and-media-services/brand-guidelines/logo-seal.html

CLIMATE, WEATHER AND GEOGRAPHY

Denver's climate is classified as semi-arid. One fascinating feature of Denver is that it is on the boundary between two major ecoregions—the Great Plains and the Rocky Mountains. This is, in part, why Denver is located where it is. Miners found it much easier to access the minerals of the mountains by following the river valleys from the Great Plains. This is also why Denver is so dry. Being on the lee, or east, side of the mountains, most of the precipitation has fallen on the west side of the Continental Divide by the time the west-to-east jet stream has flowed across the mountains.

Humidity rarely goes above 57 percent, and the city only averages approximately 15 inches of annual precipitation. Most of this precipitation is rain from summer thunderstorms, because snows are often dry with the exception of wet, spring snowstorms. Denver claims nearly three hundred days of sunshine a year. The shortest day of sunlight is around December 21, with nine hours, twenty-one minutes of daylight; the longest day is around June 21, with fourteen hours, fifty-nine minutes of daylight.

Denver's temperature is rarely below 6 degrees Fahrenheit or above 96 degrees. However, on a few occasions, Denver has reached a record high of 105. August 2020 was one of the hottest months in Denver history, with temps on seventeen out of thirty-one days soaring past 95.

The city occasionally gets ferocious downslope winds. But Denverites can also enjoy warm, light winds in the winter called Chinook winds, which can make the temperature 60 or 65 degrees in January. Along with the low humidity, it is quite possible to go outside with a very light coat on in the middle of winter. Denver's moderate winter temperatures are attractive to those who enjoy outdoor activities year-round.

Because of its dry climate, Denver has to irrigate lawns and fields. This is why the High Line Canal and other ditches run through Denver. In addition, a number of reservoirs were created around the Denver area and in the mountains to supply the city with water for residential, commercial and industrial uses. Lake Dillon Reservoir, located in Summit County, was completed in 1963. This reservoir is one of a network of reservoirs and pipelines that supply the city of Denver with water.

Because Denver is on the Great Plains, the city occasionally experiences tornadoes. Denver's most dangerous natural hazard is flash flooding, and its most destructive is hailstorms.

FURTHER EXPLORATION

Weather 5280

weather5280.com

Our Earth-Denver

youtube.com/user/geographyuberalles/search?query=denver

Weather Spark-Denver

weatherspark.com/y/3709/
Average-Weather-in-Denver-Colorado-United-States-Year-Round

Lake Dillon Reservoir

denverwater.org/recreation/dillon-resevoir

FIRES AND FLOODS

Just as Denver was starting to establish itself, fire broke out at 15th and Blake Streets in 1863, burning much of Denver's business district. Most early structures were built from native pine, so the buildings were quite flammable. The following year, in 1864, Cherry Creek flooded and water flowed through the downtown area, sweeping away buildings left after the fire. After that, Denver officials created a brick ordinance requiring new structures be built of that material instead of wood and began to rebuild the city. As a result, most of the older homes and buildings in Denver are made of brick or stone. This ordinance remained in place until approximately 1960.

More flooding from Cherry Creek occurred in 1875, 1878 and 1912. In 1933, Castlewood Dam east of Castle Rock collapsed and flooded Denver. In 1965, another flood decimated parts of Denver, killing twenty-one and resulting in millions of dollars of property damage. The 1965 flood prompted the building of Chatfield Reservoir and the Denver Urban Renewal Authority, which brought riverfront renewal to the South Platte River and Cherry Creek. Confluence Park was created as well.

FURTHER EXPLORATION

Great Fire of 1863
history.denverlibrary.org/news/
downtown-denver-burns-ground-great-fire-1863

Great Flood of 1864
history.denverlibrary.org/news/may-1864-brought-denvers-first-
big-flood-and-swept-away-much-more

Denver Flood History
mhfd.org/about/
blog/8-most-destructive-floods-in-the-denver-regions-history/

1965 Flood
coloradoencyclopedia.org/article/south-platte-flood-1965

CITY BEAUTIFUL MOVEMENT

This movement throughout the country reformed architecture and urban planning with a focus on beautification. Prior to 1901, Denver was growing and thriving, but not attractive. We can thank Denver Mayor Robert Speer for visiting the 1893 Columbian Exposition in Chicago and gaining inspiration. Speer was mayor for three terms and worked to pave streets and install sidewalks and curbs, as well as have them cleaned every night. He gave away thousands of trees for residents to plant. During Speer's first mayoral term, the Municipal Auditorium was built, and free concerts were held there on Sundays. Speer was devoted to parks, and Civic Center Park was his favorite. In addition to creating parks, he also developed a parkway system which linked existing and new parks. As you walk through Denver's first parks and drive down Speer Boulevard, you can thank Robert Speer for bringing more beauty to Denver. Lastly, he was instrumental in creating the Mountain Parks System and linking them to Denver with roads. Red Rocks Park and Amphitheatre is a perfect example.

FURTHER EXPLORATION

coloradoencyclopedia.org/article/
city-beautiful-movement-denver

coloradoencyclopedia.org/article/denver-mountain-parks

DENVER
EXPLORATION

BREWERIES
AND
RESTAURANTS

BREWERIES

Breweries are plentiful and popular in Denver. Reportedly, Denver brews more beer than any other US city. Brewery tours abound and Denver hosts the Great American Beer Festival each year.

COORS BREWERY

13th St. and Ford St., Golden, CO 80401

German immigrant Adolph Coors founded Coors Brewery in Golden in 1873. Natural spring water was and still is used today to create the brews. Coors survived eighteen years of prohibition that began in 1916 by making malted milk. The brewery is still manufacturing beer today and is open for tours. Despite its location in Golden, its age, history and location near Denver merited mention.

coors.com

TIVOLI BREWING COMPANY

900 Auraria Pkwy., Suite 240, Denver, CO 80204

Built in 1864, the brewing company is located in the Auraria neighborhood. Using an artesian well, it began brewing beer for Denver's first thirsty settlers. Heavily damaged by the Platte River flood in 1965, it closed its doors in 1969. For a while, the historic building was abandoned. Then it became a  shopping center and movie theater in the 1980s. Gradually it was converted to the Student Union of Auraria Campus of Metropolitan State University of Denver, University of Colorado Denver and Community College of Denver. In 2012, beer began to be brewed again at Tivoli, and the brewery reopened in 2015.

tivolibrewingco.com

WYNKOOP BREWING COMPANY

1634 18th St., Denver, CO 80202

Founded in 1988 in an 1800s warehouse in LoDo, this was Colorado's first brewpub. John Hickenlooper, one of the four founders, later became mayor of Denver and governor of Colorado. He brewed and served beer there before moving into politics.

wynkoop.com

FURTHER EXPLORATION

Denver Brewery List

coloradobrewerylist.com/brewery_city/denver

Great American Beer Festival

greatamericanbeerfestival.com

Beer History in Denver

denver.org/about-denver/denver-history/denver-beer-history

RESTAURANTS

There are a plethora of restaurants in Denver; for this book, the oldest and most historical ones are listed.

BUCKHORN EXCHANGE

1000 Osage St., Denver, CO 80204

Denver's oldest restaurant is the Buckhorn Exchange. It was originally named the Rio Grande Exchange and opened in 1893. It has liquor license Number One in the state of Colorado. The restaurant has catered to a wide range of people: cattlemen, miners, railroad builders, silver barons, Indian chiefs, gamblers, businessmen, celebrities and five presidents: Theodore Roosevelt, Franklin Roosevelt, Dwight Eisenhower, John F. Kennedy, Jimmy Carter and Ronald Reagan. The walls inside contain 575 taxidermy specimens of wild animals and fowl and a 125-piece gun collection. Perhaps you will try your first Rocky Mountain Oyster. Best known for steak (beef), buffalo, game and fish.

buckhorn.com

CHARLIE BROWN'S BAR AND GRILL

980 Grant St., Denver, CO 80203

Charlie Brown's Bar and Grill is part of the Colburn Hotel, which opened in 1928. The bar officially opened in 1947 when it got its liquor license. In 1964, Charlie Brown bought the bar and gave it a new name. The actor Bill Murray has been known to sing at the piano from time to time.

charliebrownsbarandgrill.com

MY BROTHER'S BAR

2376 15th St., Denver, CO 80202

My Brother's Bar has housed a bar since 1873. Originally called Highland House, its current name dates back to the 1970s when two brothers bought the establishment. Recently the restaurant was sold to Paula Newman, a waitress and general manager, who had worked there for thirty-one years. Beat Generation writers Jack Kerouac, Neal Cassady and Allen Ginsberg have all hung out there. Try a burrito and check out their two daily happy hours. Try the JCB, jalapeño cream cheese burger.

mybrothersbar.com

SAM'S NO. 3

1500 Curtis St., Denver, CO 80202

In 1927, Sam Armatas opened the first Sam's across the street from its current location, where the Federal Reserve Bank sits now. Originally, it was a nineteen-stool soda fountain. The restaurant is still family-owned. Try the Spero's breakfast burrito.

samsno3.com

ADDITIONAL RESTAURANTS

BASTIEN'S

3503 E. Colfax Ave., Denver, CO 80206

In 1937, the Bastien family purchased the Moon Drive Inn. In 1958, the old building was torn down. Mr. Bastien designed the new building, which still stands today. It is known as the home of the Sugar Steak (steak grilled with sugar).

bastiensrestaurant.com

BLUE BONNET

457 S. Broadway, Denver, CO 80209

It's one of the oldest, most authentic home-style Mexican restaurants in Denver. First opened in the 1930s after prohibition ended, it was purchased in 1968 by Arlene and Philip Mobell, and it is still a family-run restaurant.

bluebonnetrestaurant.com

CHERRY CRICKET

2641 E. 2nd Ave., Denver, CO 80206

Mary Zimmerman opened the aptly named Mary Zimmerman's Bar in Cherry Creek in 1945. Lloyd Page bought the restaurant in 1950 and changed its name to The Cherry Cricket. The rotating "Duffy's" sign was added in 1963 when Bernard Duffy took ownership and, presumably, wanted to immortalize his name. Known for their build-your-own burgers.

cherrycricket.com

GAETANO'S

3760 Tejon St., Denver, CO 80211

Opened in 1947 by the Smaldone mob family, the restaurant was popular for food and drink as well as the gambling that went on above the restaurant, which was accessible by a hidden door in the men's room. The family sold the restaurant to John Hickenlooper's Wynkoop Holdings restaurant group in 2006, but it's now back to being independently owned and operated. Known for its classic Italian dishes.

gaetanositalian.com

FURTHER EXPLORATION

Denver Restaurant List

eatdenver.com/restaurants

Rocky Mountain Oysters

en.wikipedia.org/wiki/Rocky_Mountain_oysters

CHURCHES,
CEMETERIES
AND MORTUARIES

CHURCHES

Numerous churches and places of worship are located throughout Denver. A few notable historical ones are included here to begin your exploration.

CATHEDRAL BASILICA OF THE IMMACULATE CONCEPTION

1530 Logan St., Denver, CO 80203

Construction began in 1902 and was completed in 1911. This was the first Catholic Church in Denver. Lightning bolts have struck the cathedral spires, once in 1912 and again in 1997. Pope John Paul II held mass there for World Youth Day in 1993.

denvercathedral.org

CENTRAL PRESBYTERIAN CHURCH

1660 Sherman St., Denver, CO 80203

Built in 1891, its interior includes banked, curved seating, side balconies and box seats. Great acoustics attract concerts including the Denver Philharmonic Orchestra.

centraldenver.com

EMMANUEL SHEARITH ISRAEL CHAPEL

1205 10th Street Plaza, Denver, CO 80204

Denver's oldest standing church building was constructed in 1876. Originally an Episcopal Church, it changed to a Jewish synagogue in 1903 when Shearith Israel purchased it. It remained a synagogue until 1958. It now serves as an art gallery.

emmanuelgallery.org

ST. ANDREW'S EPISCOPAL CHURCH

2015 Glenarm Pl., Denver, CO 80205

Built in 1907 at 26th and Curtis Streets and later moved to its current location, the interior contains colorful painted murals and religious sculptures.

standrewdenver.org

ST. JOHN'S CATHEDRAL

1350 Washington St., Denver, CO 80203

This cathedral was built in 1911. A pipe organ with 5,961 pipes was given to the church in honor of Denver's former mayor, Platte Rogers.

sjcathedral.org

TEMPLE EMANUEL

51 Grape St, Denver, CO 80220

Founded in 1874, it was originally located on the corner of 19th and Curtis Streets. It is the first synagogue in Colorado and the largest and oldest synagogue in the Rocky Mountain region.

emanueldenver.org

TRINITY UNITED METHODIST CHURCH

1820 Broadway,
Denver, CO 80202

Downtown Denver's first church was built in 1888. It contains an organ that is one of the finest and largest in North America. The 184-foot stone steeple is the church's crown jewel.

trinityumc.org

ZION BAPTIST CHURCH

933 E. 24th Ave., Denver, CO 80205

The oldest African American church in the Rocky Mountain region was founded in 1865. The original church was a small wood-frame structure and had been built by ex-slaves at the corner of 20th and Arapahoe Streets. In 1913, it moved to its current location.

zionbaptistchurchdenver.org

CEMETERIES AND MORTUARIES

The first organized cemetery in Denver was called Mount Prospect, later called City Cemetery. It was located on an Arapaho Indian burial ground, which today is the location of Cheesman and Congress Parks and the Denver Botanic Gardens. The first burial in 1859 was thought to be a man hung for murder.

Mount Prospect included many sections for different ethnic and religious groups. The Roman Catholic portion of the cemetery was called Mount Calvary. In 1891, Mt. Olivet Cemetery opened in Wheat Ridge. As recently as 1950, bodies were being moved from Mount Prospect to Mt. Olivet.

RIVERSIDE CEMETERY
5201 Brighton Blvd., Denver, CO 80216

Riverside Cemetery, opened in 1876, is Denver's oldest continually operating cemetery. In 1893, 788 bodies were moved from Mount Prospect to Riverside. Not all families were able to move their relatives' bodies, and so it is estimated that 4,200 bodies remain under the grass in Cheesman Park.

Riverside Cemetery has not been well-preserved. In 2003, irrigation water was turned off to the site. The cemetery is now surrounded by the industrial district of Commerce City.

fairmountfuneralhome.com/riverside-cemetery/
riverside-cemetery

FAIRMOUNT CEMETERY
430 S. Quebec St., Denver, CO 80247

Fairmount Cemetery was founded in 1890. Fairmount is filled with notables of pioneers, governors, senators, war heroes and many famous people who shaped Denver in its early days. Beautiful lawns, trees, a rose garden, wildlife, a chapel, mausoleum and art are scattered about this well-kept cemetery.

fairmountfuneralhome.com/who-we-are/
fairmount-cemetery

FORT LOGAN NATIONAL CEMETERY

4400 W Kenyon Ave., Denver, CO 80236

It was established in 1887 and contains 214 acres. Burial in a national cemetery is open to all members of the armed forces. It was named after Union General John A. Logan, who was a commander of US Volunteer forces during the American Civil War.

cem.va.gov/cems/nchp/ftlogan.asp

MT. OLIVET CEMETERY

12801 W. 44th Ave., Wheat Ridge, CO 80033

This Roman Catholic cemetery, replacing Mount Calvary, was dedicated in 1892. It is operated by the Archdiocese of Denver.

cfcscolorado.org

CROWN HILL CEMETERY

7777 W. 29th Ave., Wheat Ridge, CO 80033

Crown Hill Cemetery opened in 1907. Construction of its mausoleum named The Tower of Memories began in 1926. This building was used by pilots as a landmark to line up to land at Stapleton Airport, and it can be spotted rising above the trees from many areas west of downtown Denver.

dignitymemorial.com/funeral-homes/wheat-ridge-co/
olinger-crown-hill-mortuary-cemetery/2379

OLINGER MORTUARIES

Olinger Mortuary was founded in 1890 by John W. Olinger (1851–1901) and his wife Emma (1861–1932). It was first located on 15th and Platte Streets in Denver. In 1908, the son of John, George W. Olinger Sr., and his mother built a new building at 2600 16th Street. It was considered the first building built as a mortuary in the Rocky Mountain region. The Olingers pioneered the slumber room where the deceased person could be viewed at the mortuary instead of at home, which was a radical innovation. Five generations of the Olinger family were involved through the years of the mortuary's management. In the 1980s, all Olinger locations were sold to a large funeral home corporation. The Highland neighborhood location at 16th and Boulder Street remained a mortuary until it closed in 1999. In 2002, the former mortuary was remodeled into shops, called LoHi Marketplace, and the restaurant Linger. The Olinger sign still sits on top of the roof but the owners turned off the "O" light so it reads as Linger, and they changed "mortuaries" to "eateries."

Linger Eateries is located at 2030 W. 30th Ave., Denver, CO 80211.

lingerdenver.com

FURTHER EXPLORATION

Denver Cemeteries

history.denverlibrary.org/sites/history/files/
DenverAreaCemeteries.pdf

Denver Churches

history.denverlibrary.org/search/site/Churches

GOVERNMENT

Denver is the state capital of Colorado. Most of the government buildings are in close proximity to the capitol building.

BYRON WHITE US COURT HOUSE

1823 Stout St., Denver, CO 80257

Built between 1910 and 1916, this is a four-story marble building taking up an entire city block. It was originally called The Denver Post Office and Federal Court House. In the early 1990s, the post office moved out, the building was renovated, and in 1994, the building was renamed in honor of US Supreme Court Justice Byron White (1917–2002), a native of Fort Collins, Colorado. It is currently the seat of the United States Court of Appeals for the Tenth Circuit.

ca10.uscourts.gov/education/history/bwch-page-1

CITY AND COUNTY BUILDING

1437 Bannock St., Denver, CO 80202

Also known as City Hall, it was built in 1932. This grand building is situated on the western edge of Civic Center Park with the State Capitol building being on the eastern edge. The

completion of this building, designed by thirty-nine archi-
tects, marked the end of the City Beautiful era. The building
houses offices of the Denver mayor, City Council, Department
of Law, Public Works and Emergency Management, as well
as courtrooms for the County and District Courts. Each holiday season, the building is decorated and lighted to make it
a drive-by or walk-by destination in December and January.

COLORADO STATE CAPITOL

200 E. Colfax Ave., Denver, CO 80203

In 1881, Denver was officially chosen to be the state capital of
Colorado. It had been the temporary capital since statehood
in 1876. The capitol building was constructed in the 1890s
and opened in 1894. It was modeled after the US Capitol
building in Washington, DC. It is constructed with Colorado

white granite. Interior walls are of the rare Colorado Rose Onyx. The dome, originally copper, was gold plated in 1908. Three additional applications of gold have been applied, the last one completed in 2013. On the west steps are a few mile-high designations (5,280 feet above sea level). With different measurements, the exact step has changed, but you can see all three and pick one for a picture. Free tours are available Monday through Friday.

colorado.gov/capitol

DENVER MINT

320 W. Colfax Ave., Denver, CO 80204

If you examine your coins and see a "D" on one, it was made at the Denver Mint. The "D" can be seen under or near the date on the penny, nickel and dime, and under "In God We Trust" on the quarter. Located downtown at West Colfax and Delaware Street, the building was constructed in 1897 and started to produce coins in 1906. Adults and children seven years and older can take a tour and see the process of coin production.

usmint.gov/about/mint-tours-facilities/denver/
visiting-the-denver-mint

LEGISLATURE SERVICES BUILDING
200 E. 14th Ave., Denver, CO 80203

The building was completed in 1915 and opened as the Colorado State Museum. It remained a museum until 1976, when the collections were moved to 1300 Broadway. The building then became a legislative building due to its proximity to the Capitol.

leg.colorado.gov/agencies/
office-of-legislative-legal-services

coloradovirtuallibrary.org/
resource-sharing/state-pubs-blog/
time-machine-tuesday-the-colorado-state-museum

MCNICHOLS CIVIC CENTER BUILDING
144 W. Colfax Ave., Denver, CO 80202

Opened in 1910 as a Carnegie Library, the library outgrew its space in 1955 and moved out. The building changed its name to McNichols Civic Center Building after Stephen McNichols, Colorado's 35th governor. It's currently being used as a cultural center with spaces for events, exhibits and performances.

mcnicholsbuilding.com

HOSPITALS
AND CHARITIES

HOSPITALS

In the 1800s, tuberculosis (TB), also known as consumption, was the nation's leading cause of death. A dry climate was considered the best environment for treatment and recovery of this lung disease. People came to Denver in droves, and many sanatoriums were established here due to the favorable dry climate. The TB epidemic dissipated when antibiotics were developed to treat it in the 1940s.

TB patients enjoyed sunshine as part of their treatment.

The following hospitals are in or near Denver or were originally within Denver city limits when they were founded. Their current focus of care is included.

DENVER HEALTH, FORMERLY DENVER GENERAL HOSPITAL

777 Bannock St., Denver, CO 80204

Denver General was established in 1860. The hospital was founded near 11th and Wazee, but in 1873, a new medical center was built at the corner of 6th Avenue and Cherokee. The hospital was well-known for founding the first nursing school west of the Mississippi and for being one of the earliest facilities to treat tuberculosis. Denver Health is a comprehensive hospital that provides emergency care. It is Colorado's primary safety-net institution.

denverhealth.org

FITZSIMONS ARMY MEDICAL CENTER

13001 E. 17th Pl., Aurora, CO 80045

Open from 1918 to 1996, this hospital, which was initially called Army Hospital 21, opened during World War I to treat soldiers with tuberculous and those exposed to chemical weapons during the war. In 1920, it was renamed in honor of Lt. William T. Fitzsimons, the first American medical officer killed in World War I. The facility was also used heavily in World War II. President Dwight Eisenhower was treated there three times, and his suite where he recovered from a heart attack is preserved and viewable today by appointment. The building is now part of Anschutz Medical Campus and is being redeveloped into a research campus.

coloradoencyclopedia.org/article/
fitzsimons-general-hospital

NATIONAL JEWISH HOSPITAL

1400 Jackson St., Denver, CO 80206

Founded in 1899 to treat tuberculosis, it is now known as a respiratory hospital and offers treatment and research for pulmonary, cardiac and immune-related conditions.

nationaljewish.org

PORTER MEMORIAL/PORTER ADVENTIST HOSPITAL

2525 S. Downing St., Denver, CO 80210

Opened in 1930, it currently specializes in joint replacement, spine surgery, organ transplant, behavioral health, cancer care and innovative cardiac treatments.

centura.org/locations/porter-adventist-hospital

PRESBYTERIAN / ST. LUKE'S MEDICAL CENTER

1719 E. 19th Ave., Denver, CO 80218

St. Luke's Hospital opened in 1891 and closed in 1992. At the closing, patients were moved to nearby Presbyterian Hospital, which opened in 1926. The hospital is highly rated in emergency, pediatric, cancer, high-risk pregnancy and bone marrow transplant services.

pslmc.com

ST. ANTHONY HOSPITAL

11600 W. 2nd Pl., Lakewood, CO 80228

The hospital was previously located at W. 16th Ave. and Raleigh Street.

Opened in 1892, it is one of three Level 1 Trauma Centers in Colorado. In 1972, it was the first hospital in the nation to launch the civilian hospital air ambulance service, Flight For Life.

centura.org/locations/st-anthony-hospital

SAINT JOSEPH HOSPITAL

1375 19th Ave., Denver, CO 80218

The Sisters of Charity of Leavenworth, Kansas, founded Saint Joseph Hospital in Denver in 1873. It was the first private hospital in Colorado. Today, it continues as the largest private teaching hospital in Denver. It specializes in cardiology, mom/baby care and oncology.

sclhealth.org/locations/saint-joseph-hospital

CU ANSCHUTZ MEDICAL CAMPUS

1635 Aurora Ct., Aurora, CO 80045

This hospital is listed last since it is the newest and also not in Denver proper. The campus was founded in 2006, and several of Denver's downtown hospitals, such as Children's Hospital Colorado and UCHealth University of Colorado Hospital, have relocated to it. The University of Colorado Health Sciences Center had been located on 9th Avenue in Denver but moved to this campus in 2016. The University of Colorado has six health science-related schools and colleges on the campus.

cuanschutz.edu

FURTHER EXPLORATION

Tuberculosis

history.com/news/
the-disease-that-helped-put-colorado-on-the-map

9news.com/article/news/local/morning-show/history-colorado-tuberculosis-exhibit-national-jewish/73-0cde941f-d169-4982-adf2-171a161cfd05

CHARITIES

Early in Denver's history, charity-minded individuals began to create societies, organizations and homes for those in need.

LADIES' UNION AID SOCIETY

The first known charitable organization in Denver was founded in 1860 by Elizabeth "Libby" Byers (1834–1920). Originally, the group assisted the poor and made clothes and bandages for Colorado Civil War soldiers. In 1874, Margaret Gray Evans joined Byers' efforts and helped reorganize as the Ladies' Relief Society and together built the Old Ladies' Home on West 38th Avenue.

HEBREW LADIES BENEVOLENT SOCIETY

This society was established in 1872 to service Denver's Jewish early residents. Frances Wisebart Jacobs (1843–1892) led this society's organization. In 1887, she formed Charity Organization Society and later was a co-founder of United Way of America. She also established Denver's Jewish Hospital Association.

jewishfamilyservice.org/about-jfs/history

en.wikipedia.org/wiki/Frances_Wisebart_Jacobs

JEWISH CONSUMPTIVES' RELIEF SOCIETY (JCRS)

This society was founded in 1904 to treat those with tuberculous free of charge at any stage of the disease, regardless of their ethnicity or religious affiliation. A JCRS hospital was established at West Colfax and Pierce Streets. In 1954 as TB was being treated effectively with antibiotics, the institution changed its name to American Medical Center and in the 1970s to AMC Cancer Research Center and Hospital.

jgsco.org/cpage.php?pt=56

ARGYLE, FORMERLY OLD LADIES' HOME

4115 W. 38th Ave., Denver, CO 80212

Originally built in 1874 and named the Old Ladies' Home, the Argyle is currently an assisted and independent living community for seniors.

theargyle.org

DENVER CHILDREN'S HOME, FORMERLY DENVER ORPHANS' HOME

1501 Albion St., Denver, CO 80220

It was established in 1881 as an orphanage to provide shelter for children in need, and Margaret Evans was instrumental in its organization. In 1902, it moved to its current location and has operated as the Denver Children's Home since 1962.

denverchildrenshome.org

DENVER RESCUE MISSION

Denver's oldest full-service charity serves homeless men, women and children by providing food, shelter and life-changing programs. It was established in 1892 as Market Street Mission, a home for former prostitutes. Joshua Gravett opened this home to see broken lives restored. It now includes multiple locations and services.

denverrescuemission.org

FURTHER EXPLORATION

Colorado Gives / Community First Foundation was established in 2007 as an online giving tool. Many current Denver charity organizations can be found there.

coloradogives.org

HOTELS

Hotels of all types and styles are located in Denver, and this section highlights some older ones with historical relevance.

BROWN PALACE HOTEL

321 17th St., Denver, CO 80202

Opened in 1892, this hotel was built to provide luxury and elegance to travelers. Placed on a triangular plot, the building is distinctive with a stunning lobby and four restaurants. It has hosted presidents, foreign royalty and a variety of famous people. Afternoon tea is a way to soak in the hotel and its splendor. The yearly Denver Debutante Ball is quite a spectacle as young ladies are presented to Denver Society.

brownpalace.com

OXFORD HOTEL

1600 17th St., Denver, CO 80202

Opened in 1891, this is Denver's oldest hotel that still remains in operation. This hotel was quite opulent and luxurious when it opened. It was renovated in the 1920s in an art deco-style makeover. The famous Cruise Room was added, which was modeled after a lounge on the Queen Mary ship. It was renovated again in the 1980s to restore it to its former glory as a cherished, beautiful historic hotel in Denver.

theoxfordhotel.com

ROSSONIAN HOTEL

2642 Welton St., Denver, CO 80205

Built in 1907, it opened in 1912 as the Baxter Hotel and was renamed in 1929 as the Rossonian Hotel. Located in the Five Points neighborhood, the hotel and lounge attracted musicians such as Duke Ellington, Count Basie, Nat King Cole, Billie Holiday and Ella Fitzgerald. It became a hot spot for jazz. It is currently not in use but may be refurbished in the future.

coloradoencyclopedia.org/article/rossonian-hotel

OLD BUILDINGS THAT HAVE BEEN CONVERTED TO HOTELS

COURTYARD BY MARRIOTT DENVER DOWNTOWN

934 16th St. Mall, Denver, CO 80202

It's located in the historic Tritch / Joslins Dry Goods Building, which was erected in 1887.

marriott.com/hotels/travel/
dencd-courtyard-denver-downtown

CRAWFORD HOTEL

1701 Wynkoop St., Denver, CO 80202

Located inside Denver Union Station, this hotel opened in 2014 and is named after urban preservationist Dana Crawford.

thecrawfordhotel.com

HOTEL MONACO

1717 Champa St., Denver, CO 80202

Originally built in 1876, the hotel was built in 1998 inside the renovated 1917 Railroad Exchange Building and 1928 Art Moderne Title Building.

monaco-denver.com

HOTEL TEATRO

1100 14th St., Denver, CO 80202

Located in the 1911 Denver Tramway Building, the hotel was created in 1999.

hotelteatro.com

MAGNOLIA HOTEL

818 17th St., Denver, CO 80202

Built in 1911, it is located in First National Bank / American National Bank building. This building is famously known as Denver's first skyscraper.

marriott.com/hotels/travel/
denmg-magnolia-hotel-denver-a-tribute-portfolio-hotel

PATTERSON HISTORIC INN

420 E. 11th Ave.,
Denver, CO 80203

Constructed in 1891, it was originally a private home in Denver's high-end neighborhood that was referred to as Millionaire's Row. The house was sold to Thomas M. Patterson in 1892. Patterson was a congressman, senator and editor and publisher of the *Rocky Mountain News*. The regal mansion has been well-maintained and is designated as a National Historic Landmark.

pattersoninn.com/en-us

RENAISSANCE DENVER DOWNTOWN CITY CENTER

918 17th St., Denver, CO 80202

It is located in the Colorado National Bank building originally constructed in 1915. Old bank vaults can be viewed in the lounge overlooking the lobby and murals.

marriott.com/hotels/travel/
dendr-renaissance-denver-downtown-city-center-hotel

FURTHER EXPLORATION

Historical Hotels of Denver

denver.org/denver-hotels/unique-denver-hotels/historic-hotels

LANDMARKS AND IMPORTANT BUILDINGS

This section includes landmarks and important buildings expanded upon or not listed in other sections.

CABLELAND

4150 E. Shangri La Dr., Denver, CO 80246

Official residence of the mayor of Denver, this home is located in the Hilltop neighborhood.

cableland.org

COLORADO NATIONAL BANK BUILDING

918 17th St., Denver, CO 80202

It was built in 1915 and located on 17th Street in the financial district of Denver, which was dubbed "Wall Street of the Rockies." It has gained multiple contemporary additions through the years. The sixteen large murals surrounding the lobby are titled "Indian Memories" and were painted by renowned Colorado artist Allen Tupper True in 1925. The building hosted a bank until 2007. In 2011, it converted to a 230-room boutique hotel. It is currently called the Renaissance Denver Downtown City Center Hotel.

renewdenver.org/projects/colorado-national-bank

DENVER GAS AND ELECTRIC BUILDING
910 15th St., Denver, CO 80202

Denver's grandest illuminated building was built in 1910. It rises ten stories and is adorned with thirteen thousand electric light bulbs. Denver Gas and Electric became Public Service Company and eventually moved out. The building was renamed the Insurance Exchange. Currently, it houses telecommunication companies.

910telecom.com/history

DENVER TRAMWAY COMPANY POWERHOUSE

1416 Platte St.,
Denver, CO 80202

Founded in 1886, it powered
Denver's streetcar network. At the height of its trolley operations, the tramway operated over 250 streetcars and 160 miles of track. As automobiles became more popular, it closed in 1950. The building was repurposed a number of times until Recreational Equipment Inc. (REI) bought and renovated it, opening in 2000.

en.wikipedia.org/wiki/Denver_Tramway

rei.com/stores/denver.html

DENVER PRESS CLUB

1330 Glenarm Pl., Denver, CO 80204

Denver journalists first gathered as a press club in 1867 and incorporated as the Denver Press Club in 1877 as the oldest press club in the United States. The club moved to this building in 1925. A mural of Denver journalists was painted in 1945 in the basement poker room, where it remains today.

denverpressclub.org

DENVER WOMAN'S PRESS CLUB

1325 Logan St., Denver, CO 80203

The DWPC was founded in 1898 by nineteen charter members. In 1924, the DWPC purchased the studio home of George Elbert Burr, an artist famous for his etchings of Colorado. The clubhouse is the only structure on its side of the block now and is a historic landmark. The Denver Woman's Press Club is a professional membership organization that supports women in journalism, media, communications and literary fields.

dwpconline.org

GOVERNOR'S MANSION

400 E. 8th Ave., Denver, CO 80203

Completed in 1908, the building is also known as the Cheesman-Boettcher Mansion. Walter Cheesman commissioned the house in Capitol Hill to be constructed but died before it was finished. After Mrs. Cheesman died in 1923, Claude Boettcher purchased it. The mansion was left to the Boettcher Foundation after his death. It has been available for residential use by governors since 1960. It is also available for scheduled tours.

governor-residence.colorado.gov/history

MUSEUMS AND LIBRARIES

MUSEUMS

Art, history and many treasures are contained within Denver's museums.

AMERICAN MUSEUM OF WESTERN ART

1727 Tremont Pl., Denver, CO 80202

Founded in 2010, this nonprofit museum is the permanent home for The Anschutz Collection, a formerly private collection of paintings that surveys the art of the American West from the early 19th century to the present.

anschutzcollection.org

BLACK AMERICAN WEST MUSEUM

3091 California St., Denver, CO 80205

The former home of Dr. Justina Ford, the first Black woman doctor in Denver, hosts this museum. The museum is filled with artifacts that tell the story of African American men and women who helped settle and develop the American West.

bawmhc.org

CENTER FOR WOMEN'S HISTORY AT BYERS–EVANS HOUSE

1310 Bannock St., Denver, CO 80204

William Byers, founder of the *Rocky Mountain News*, built what is now known as the Byers–Evans House Museum in 1883. It was sold to William Gray Evans in 1889. In 1981, the house and its contents were donated to the Colorado Historical Society. The house has been restored to the 1912–1924 period and includes approximately 90 percent of the original furniture, glassware, china and other household items belonging to the Evans family.

The Center for Colorado Women's History at the Byers–Evans House Museum focuses on scholarship, research, lectures, tours and exhibits that expand the understanding and collective memory of the history of women in Colorado.

historycolorado.org/
center-colorado-womens-history-byers-evans-house

CHILDREN'S MUSEUM OF DENVER
2121 Children's Museum Dr., Denver, CO 80211

The museum was founded in June 1973 in a traveling bus. In 1975, the museum moved into a renovated building on Bannock Street and then moved to its current location along the South Platte River in 1984. In the spring of 2014, the Children's Museum of Denver began an expansion. Following several years of planning and two years of construction, the expansion doubled the size of the museum and included eight additional exhibits, one outdoor and seven indoor. The expanded museum reopened its doors in 2015 as the Children's Museum of Denver at Marsico Campus.

The museum focuses on early childhood education, serving children newborn through age eight and their caregivers by offering interactive exhibits and educational programming. Its core early learning focus areas include science, technology, engineering and math (STEM), health and wellness, 21st century skills, literacy and the arts.

mychildsmuseum.org

CLYFFORD STILL MUSEUM

1250 Bannock St., Denver, CO 80204

Opened in 2011, the museum allows visitors the unique experience to understand the legacy of Clyfford Still (1904–1980), an artist whose life had been shrouded in mystery. The bulk of his work had been hidden from public view for more than thirty years. Considered one of the most important painters of the 20th century, Still was among the first generation of abstract expressionist artists who developed a new and powerful approach to painting in the years immediately following World War II.

clyffordstillmuseum.org

DENVER ART MUSEUM

100 W. 14th Ave. Pkwy., Denver, CO 80204

The Denver Art Museum is one of the largest art museums between the West Coast and Chicago. The museum's origins can be traced back to the founding of the Denver Artists Club in 1893. The Club renamed itself the Denver Art Association in 1917 and, in 1923, the Denver Art Association became the Denver Art Museum (DAM). In 1948, the DAM purchased a building on Acoma and 14th Avenue on the south side of Civic Center Park. Denver architect Burnham Hoyt renovated the building, which opened as the Schleier Memorial Gallery in 1949. In 1954, the South Wing (now known as the Bach Wing) opened. The North Building, a seven-story, 210,000-square-foot addition, opened in 1971, allowing the museum to finally display its collections under one roof. The

Duncan Pavilion and the Frederic C. Hamilton Building were both added to the museum in 2006. The Duncan Pavilion, a 5,700-square-foot, second-story addition to the Bach Wing, received the bridge traffic from the new Hamilton Building and the existing North Building.

denverartmuseum.org

DENVER FIREFIGHTERS MUSEUM
1326 Tremont Pl., Denver, CO 80204

This museum was established in 1978 and is located in former Fire Station Number One, which was built in 1909. Its collection preserves the history of the Denver Fire Department and firefighting as well as educating the public on fire safety.

denverfirefightersmuseum.org

DENVER MUSEUM OF NATURE AND SCIENCE
2001 Colorado Blvd., Denver, CO 80205

In 1868, Edwin Carter moved into a tiny cabin in Breckenridge, Colorado, to pursue his passion: the scientific study of the birds and mammals of the Rocky Mountains. Almost single-handedly, Carter assembled one of the most complete collections of Colorado fauna then in existence.

Word of Carter's collection spread and, in 1892, a group of prominent Denver citizens declared their interest in moving his collection to the capital city for all to see. Carter offered to sell the entire collection for $10,000. The founders also secured a collection of butterflies and moths and a collection of crystallized gold.

Together, these three collections formed the nucleus of what would become the Colorado Museum of Natural History, officially incorporated in 1900. After years of preparation and construction, the Colorado Museum of Natural History finally opened to the public in 1908.

The city of Denver increased its funding for the museum, leading to a name change to Denver Museum of Natural History in 1948. In 2000, the name was changed to the present Denver Museum of Nature and Science to reflect the institution's wider focus. In addition to exhibits, the museum also contains Gates Planetarium and Phipps IMAX Theater.

dmns.org

FORNEY MUSEUM OF TRANSPORTATION
4303 Brighton Blvd., Denver, CO 80216

The Forney Museum of Transportation began as the private collection of J. D. Forney of Fort Collins, Colorado. From an early age, Forney had an interest in cars, airplanes and all modes of transportation. Today, it includes not just vehicles, but also buggies, motorcycles, steam locomotives, aircraft, carriages, rail equipment, fire apparatus, public transportation, sleighs, bicycles, toys and die cast models and vintage apparel.

forneymuseum.org

FOUR MILE HISTORIC PARK

715 S. Forest St., Denver, CO 80246

This 12-acre park is the site of Denver's oldest house. The Pioneer museum and park includes a log home, a barn with farm animals and guided tours.

fourmilepark.org

HISTORY COLORADO CENTER

1200 N. Broadway, Denver, CO 80203

The History Colorado Center is a museum dedicated to the history of the state of Colorado. Its predecessor, the Colorado History Museum, closed in 2010 and the current museum opened in 2012. The History Colorado Center features six permanent exhibits: Living West, Colorado Stories, Denver

A–Z, Destination Colorado, Time Machine, and Denver Diorama. All exhibits feature hands-on opportunities for childhood learning and interesting displays for adults.

historycolorado.org/history-colorado-center

KIRKLAND MUSEUM OF FINE AND DECORATIVE ART

1201 Bannock St., Denver, CO 80204

At this museum, you can view over 4,400 works of art. You may also see the original studio and art school building of artist Vance Kirkland. It opened to the public in 2003, displaying the works of Kirkland, his Colorado and regional colleagues, and international decorative art. In 2014, the museum relocated to its current location.

kirklandmuseum.org

MIZEL MUSEUM

400 S. Kearney St., Denver, CO 80224

This museum, opened in 1982, highlights Jewish history, exhibits and cultural events. Tours are by appointment only.

mizelmuseum.org

MOLLY BROWN HOUSE MUSEUM

1340 Pennsylvania St.,
Denver CO 80203

This was the home of Margaret Brown, who was a philanthropist, activist and socialite. She was better known as "The Unsinkable Molly Brown" because she survived the sinking of the RMS Titanic. She acquired the home in Capitol Hill in 1894. After her death in 1932, the house was altered into twelve separate spaces for roomers and boarders and later served as a home for girls. In 1970, the house was saved from demolition and restored to the original Victorian grandeur. It is open for tours and special events.

mollybrown.org

MUSEO DE LAS AMERICAS-LATIN AMERICAN ART MUSEUM

861 Santa Fe Dr., Denver, CO 80204

This museum is dedicated to educating the community through collecting, preserving, interpreting and exhibiting the diverse arts and cultures of the Americas, from ancient to contemporary. The museum offers innovative exhibitions and programs.

museo.org

MUSEUM OF CONTEMPORARY ART DENVER

1485 Delgany St., Denver, CO 80202

The Museum of Contemporary Art Denver (MCA Denver) explores the art and culture of our time through rotating exhibits and public educational programs. Featuring regional, national and international artists, MCA Denver offers a wide range of exhibits promoting creative experimentation with art and ideas. MCA Denver was founded in 1996 and moved to its current location in 2007.

mcadenver.org

WINGS OVER THE ROCKIES AIR AND SPACE MUSEUM

7711 E. Academy Blvd., Denver, CO 80230

Established in 1994 on the former Lowry Air Force Base, the museum preserves the history of the base's operations (1938–1994) and features multiple aircraft exhibits. It also hosts events and educational opportunities.

wingsmuseum.org

LIBRARIES

In 1878, books were donated and maintained in the south wing of Denver East High School. Denver Public Library was officially established in 1889. In 1910, the library moved to its own building in Civic Center Park. That original building still stands and is now called McNichols Civic Center Building. There are twenty-five branch library locations in addition to Central Library in Denver.

CENTRAL LIBRARY

10 W. 14th Ave. Pkwy., Denver, CO 80204

This library opened in 1956 as a Carnegie library. Andrew Carnegie (1835–1919), American industrialist and financier, contributed to the building of over 2,500 public libraries throughout the English-speaking world. Almost 1,700 of these were in the United States, with thirty-six in Colorado. Between 1913 and 1920, Carnegie underwrote construction of Denver's first eight branches:

Ford-Warren Branch
2825 N. High St., Denver, CO 80205 (1913)

Decker Branch Library
1500 S. Logan St., Denver, CO 80210 (1913)

Woodbury Branch

3265 Federal Blvd., Denver, CO 80211 (1913)

Dickinson Branch

1550 Hooker St., Denver, CO (1913): closed in 1954, currently vacant.

Smiley Branch Library

4501 W. 46th Ave., Denver, CO 80212 (1918)

Byers Branch

675 Santa Fe Dr., Denver, CO 80204 (1918)

Elyria Branch

4725 N. High St., Denver, CO (1920): closed in 1952, currently a private residence.

Park Hill Branch

4705 Montview Blvd., Denver, CO 80207 (1920)

Four Ross branches were funded by Denver real estate investor and library commissioner, Frederick Ross:

Ross-Broadway

33 E. Bayaud Ave., Denver, CO 80209 (1951)

Ross-Barnum

3570 W. First Ave., Denver, CO 80219 (1954)

Ross-University Hills
4310 E. Amherst Ave., Denver, CO 80222 (1962)

Ross-Cherry Creek
305 Milwaukee St., Denver, CO 80206 (1962)

BLAIR-CALDWELL AFRICAN AMERICAN RESEARCH LIBRARY
2401 Welton St., Denver, CO 80205

This library, opened in 2003, was named after two prominent activists: Omar Blair, the first Black president of Denver Public Schools Board of Education (from 1972 to 1984) and Elvin Caldwell, first Black Denver City Council member (from 1955 to 1980).

Additional locations:
denverlibrary.org/locations

Additional history:
history.denverlibrary.org/history-denver-public-library

NEIGHBORHOODS AND SWALLOWED TOWNS

NEIGHBORHOODS

Early in Denver's history, many neighborhoods became known for their wealthy inhabitants, who were predominantly white, Anglo-Saxon Protestant Americans. Denver also had many working-class and laboring-class citizens of various backgrounds and ethnicities. One of the earliest groups of non-English-speaking laborers were German. They were the first to found an ethnic organization, the Denver Turnverein, in 1866. Italians arrived to work on the railroad, and the Chinese arrived, who also primarily worked as servants, janitors and laundry operators.

A Jewish community and an African American community

settled in Denver. Spanish-speaking immigrants worked season-
ally on nearby farms and eventually established themselves within
Denver as well. Sadly, these groups were not always treated well.
Segregation and ill treatment of minorities gradually diminished
with the civil rights movement but have not been eliminated and still
remain an issue in need of improvement today.

Denver has approximately seventy-eight neighborhoods, depend-
ing on which resource you reference. The popularity of nicknames
and separate identities for neighborhoods will likely grow this list in
the future. Enjoy this summary of some of the communities within
Denver city limits that have the most history or landmarks. I have
gathered a few highlights and highly suggest further exploration to
learn more about each area.

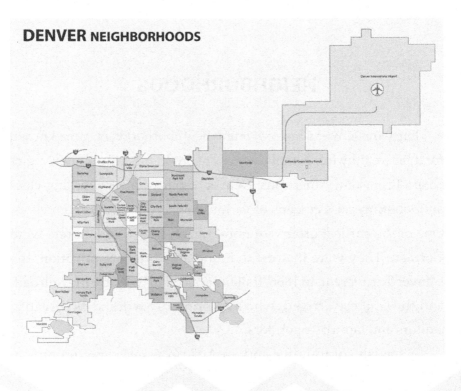

DENVER NEIGHBORHOODS

AURARIA

Part of Denver's original settlement, Auraria is located on the banks of Cherry Creek and the South Platte River. In the 1920s, Hispanic people largely lived in this neighborhood, expanding to the west and north over time. It is now known for the campus of the Auraria Higher Education Center (AHEC) that opened in 1976. It is the home to the University of Colorado Denver, Metropolitan State University of Denver, and the Community College of Denver. Tivoli Brewery is also located in Auraria. A former Israeli prime minister, Golda Meir, resided from 1969 to 1974 in a home in Auraria that can be visited today as a museum. Ninth Street Historic Park, located on 9th between Champa and Curtis Streets, hosts some of the oldest homes in Denver.

history.denverlibrary.org/auraria-neighborhood

BAKER

This area is located in the inner southwest part of Denver proper. The Byers family established themselves here. William Byers founded the *Rocky Mountain News* newspaper in 1859. The paper ceased publication in 2009. West High School, the Mayan Theatre and Blue Bonnet restaurant are all located in the Baker neighborhood.

history.denverlibrary.org/neighborhood-history-guide/
baker-neighborhood-history

CAPITOL HILL

Denver's wealthiest citizens once called Capitol Hill home. It contains the Capitol building and many centuries-old mansions, including the Molly Brown House. At one time, Millionaire's Row, with its impressive houses, was the place to reside. When Colfax Avenue was zoned commercial in the 1920s, many of the mansions were converted to offices or apartments or demolished to create new apartment or office buildings and parking lots. The Sherman Historic District in the Capitol Hill neighborhood consists of three-story brick apartments on the 1000 block of Sherman between 10th and 11th Avenues. The apartment buildings are known as "Poet's Row" because they are named after literary figures.

history.denverlibrary.org/capitol-hill-neighborhood-history

CHERRY CREEK

Harman was the original name of this town, which is now known for Denver's first shopping center and upscale Cherry Creek North, which contains high-end boutique shopping. Many affluent homes surround this area. Before the shopping center was created, the area was a garbage dump.

history.denverlibrary.org/neighborhood-history-guide/ cherry-creek-neighborhood

CURTIS PARK

This area includes Denver's oldest neighborhood and first streetcar suburb. Early Denver residents wanted to expand away from the city center and moved east to this neighborhood. Many old homes still exist here, as well as Temple Emanuel Synagogue.

history.denverlibrary.org/
curtis-park-denvers-oldest-neighborhood-upgrade

EAST 7TH AVENUE

This historic district contains many mansions, including the Governor's Mansion.

history.denverlibrary.org/east-7th-avenue-historic-district

EAST COLFAX

East Colfax includes the legendary Colfax Avenue as well as these landmarks mentioned within this book:

- State Capitol
- Cathedral of the Immaculate Conception
- National Jewish Hospital
- East High School
- City Park
- Mammoth / Fillmore Auditorium
- Ogden Theatre

- Bonfils/Lowenstein Theatre / Tattered Cover Book Store
- Bastien's Restaurant

history.denverlibrary.org/east-colfax-neighborhood

FIVE POINTS

In 1881, Five Points was named for the five-way diagonal intersection of Welton Street, 27th Street, Washington Street and 26th Avenue. African Americans were the prominent occupants of this neighborhood, and Five Points became the heart of the Black community. Jazz and blues musicians often played at the Rossonian Hotel and other venues. Fire Station No. 3 in Five Points was the first all-Black fire station in Denver. The Zion Baptist Church and the Temple Emanuel were both established there. It is informally known as Harlem of the West.

history.denverlibrary.org/
five-points-whittier-neighborhood-history

GLOBEVILLE

Globeville was originally platted in 1889 and was incorporated as a town in 1891. Denver annexed it in 1902. Globe Smelting and Refining Company was located there, and many immigrants from eastern European countries worked and lived in this community. In addition to smelters, other employers included the railroad, foundries, brickyards and meat-packing plants. Today, I-25 and I-70 bisect the neighborhood. This diverse community was and continues to be filled with stories rich in the history and culture of Denver.

historycolorado.org/globeville-elyria-swansea

HIGHLAND

Highland was originally a city in its own right, incorporating in 1875. In 1896, Highland was annexed to Denver. It is the home of Olinger's (Linger Eatery) and North High School.

history.denverlibrary.org/
potter-highlands-neighborhood-history

LODO (LOWER DOWNTOWN)

This original settlement of Denver evolved into a warehouse district. This area gradually declined until it became a bit sketchy in the 1980s. Thanks to urban revitalization, it has become a popular hot spot today, with many restored and repurposed buildings. It is now filled with offices, lofts, restaurants, shops and galleries, and contains many landmarks such as Union Station, the Oxford Hotel, Wynkoop Brewery and Coors Field.

history.denverlibrary.org/
lodo-denvers-lower-downtown-success-story

PARK HILL

Platted in 1887, the area previously contained dairy farms. East of City Park, it offered a residential buffer to the noise and bustle of the downtown area. Stapleton International Airport (1929–1995) was located next to the Park Hill neighborhood. It closed when the new Denver International Airport was built in 1995.

history.denverlibrary.org/park-hill-neighborhood-history

SLOAN'S LAKE

In 1861, this lake was created when a farmer tapped into an aquifer. It gradually became a recreational attraction to Denver. In 1891, Manhattan Beach, Denver's first amusement park, opened on the north shore. It closed in 1914. St. Anthony Hospital used to be located in this neighborhood until it relocated to Lakewood.

history.denverlibrary.org/sloans-lake-neighborhood-history

UNIVERSITY PARK

Originally a potato farm, this area is now the home of University of Denver. The university completed Chamberlin Observatory in 1891 and installed it in what is now Observatory Park.

history.denverlibrary.org/
university-park-neighborhood-history

WASHINGTON PARK

Smith Lake was created in 1867 and was primarily used for ice production. Denver's first bathing beach opened in 1911 on Smith Lake's north shore. A bathhouse and pavilion were built for swimming in the summer and ice-skating in the winter. Swimming was originally a segregated activity for whites only. Multiple protests surrounding this issue occurred over the years. Swimming ceased in 1957 due to the polio epidemic. The town in this area was originally called South Denver. In 1897, the area was annexed to Denver. South High School is located in this neighborhood.

history.denverlibrary.org/washington-park-neighborhood

WEST COLFAX

Originally, this neighborhood was home to Denver's Jewish population. The neighborhood contained hospitals such as Beth Israel Hospital and the Jewish Consumptives' Relief Society Sanatorium to help tuberculosis patients. Multiple synagogues and schools were built for the community. Now the area is predominantly Hispanic, Asian and multi-ethnic.

history.denverlibrary.org/
west-colfax-neighborhood-history

NEIGHBORHOOD COMMERCIAL DISTRICTS / FORMER STREETCAR COMMERCIAL STRIPS

There areas of Denver have small commercial blocks that were formerly streetcar stops. Those rail lines have been removed, but retail stores, restaurants, commercial office space, festivals and events still exist today at those former stops.

Highland Square: visitdenverhighlands.com
South Gaylord Street: oldsouthgaylord.com
Old South Pearl Street: southpearlstreet.com
Tennyson Street: shoptennyson.com

LIST OF NEIGHBORHOODS

CENTRAL NEIGHBORHOODS

Baker

Capitol Hill

Central Business District

Cheesman Park

Cherry Creek

City Park

City Park West

Civic Center

Congress Park

Country Club

Lincoln Park

North Capitol Hill

Speer

Union Station

EAST NEIGHBORHOODS

Belcaro

Cory-Merrill

East Colfax

Hale

Hilltop

Indian Creek

Lowry

Montclair

Park Hill

Virginia Village

Washington Virginia Vale

Windsor

NORTH NEIGHBORHOODS

Clayton

Cole

Elyria-Swansea

Five Points

Globeville

North Park Hill

Skyland

South Park Hill

Whittier

NORTHEAST NEIGHBORHOODS

Central Park *(formerly Stapleton)*

Denver International Airport

Gateway / Green Valley Ranch

Montbello

Northeast Park Hill

NORTHWEST NEIGHBORHOODS

Auraria

Berkeley

Chaffee Park

Highland

Jefferson Park

Regis

Sloan Lake

Sunnyside

West Highland

SOUTH NEIGHBORHOODS

College View / South Platte

Overland

Platt Park

Rosedale

University

University Hills

University Park

Washington Park

Washington Park West

Wellshire

SOUTHEAST NEIGHBORHOODS

Goldsmith

Hampden

Hampden South

Kennedy

Southmoor Park

SOUTHWEST NEIGHBORHOODS

Bear Valley

Fort Logan

Harvey Park

Harvey Park South

Marston

WEST NEIGHBORHOODS

Athmar Park

Barnum

Barnum West

Mar Lee

Ruby Hill

Sun Valley

Valverde

Villa Park

West Colfax

Westwood

NON-OFFICIAL NEIGHBORHOODS

Alamo Placita: *a historic district, part of the larger Speer neighborhood.*

Burns Brentwood

Crestmoor

Curtis Park

Golden Triangle: *an area which incorporates many of Denver's civic and cultural institutions; roughly corresponds with the Civic Center neighborhood.*

Hampden Heights

LoDo: *original settlement of Denver with many of its oldest buildings and is known for its nightlife. Overlaps with parts of Union Station and Five Points neighborhoods.*

Mayfair

Northside

Parkfield

RiNo *(River North Art District)*

Uptown: *roughly corresponds with North Capitol Hill neighborhood.*

FURTHER EXPLORATION

City and County of Denver Official Site of Neighborhoods
denvergov.org/content/denvergov/en/community-planning-and-development/planning-and-design/completed-plans/denver-statistical-neighborhoods.html

Neighborhood Map
denvergov.org/media/gis/WebDocs/Citywide/Neighborhoods.pdf

Denver Library Neighborhood History
history.denverlibrary.org/neighborhoods

Further Neighborhood Information
en.wikipedia.org/wiki/List_of_neighborhoods_in_Denver

kdvr.com/2017/04/19/denvers-neighborhood-nicknames

uncovercolorado.com/best-neighborhoods-in-denver-co

Walking Denver's Neighborhoods
denverbyfoot.com/books

SWALLOWED TOWNS—NOW SUBURBS

Some of Denver's suburbs used to be separate towns, but over time, they were swallowed in suburban growth. There are many suburbs of Denver, but included here are only those with traditional downtown areas.

ARVADA

This town is located eight miles northwest of central Denver. The area's earliest documented gold discovery was in 1850 on Ralston Creek. In 1870, Benjamin Franklin Wadsworth founded the town. While visiting Olde Town Arvada, which is listed on the National Register of Historic Places, stop and enjoy the restaurants and shops. Olde Town is bounded by Ralston Road, Teller Road, Grandview Avenue and Yukon Street.

arvadahistory.org

ENGLEWOOD

Englewood is located seven miles south of central Denver. Gold was discovered in Little Dry Creek in 1858. In 1860, the town was founded with the name Orchard Place. In 1883, the Cherrelyn horsecar path was laid, later becoming Cherrelyn Trolley, which ran until 1908. In 1905, the Swedish National Sanatorium was founded for treatment of tuberculosis (now Swedish Medical Center). In 1965, Cinderella City opened, which at the time was the largest shopping mall west of the Mississippi River. The original downtown area was on South Broadway at the intersection of Hampden Avenue.

englewoodco.gov/our-community/englewood-history

GOLDEN

In 1859, twelve miles west of central Denver, the town of Golden City was founded by prospector Thomas L. Golden. Between 1862 and 1867, it was Colorado's territorial capital. Coors Brewing Company was founded in 1873, and Colorado School of Mines was founded in 1874. Visit charming Washington Avenue and its surrounding blocks for restaurants and shops.

cityofgolden.net/live/golden-history

LITTLETON

In 1867, ten miles south of central Denver, Rough and Ready Flour Mill opened. In 1890, the town was founded by Richard Sullivan Little. Visit charming Main Street for restaurants and shops, beautifully decorated at Christmastime.

littletongov.org/my-littleton/littleton-history/
general-history

PARKS AND WATER

PARKS

The City Beautiful Movement was a part of North American architecture and urban planning in the 1890s and 1900s. In Denver, Robert W. Speer endorsed this project, envisioning and implementing many parks and monuments to take Denver from a cow town to an impressive city. The Civic Center, comprised of the State Capitol building on one end and the City and County Building on the other, is an example of this planning.

Most Denver neighborhoods have parks within them. Included here are a few of the larger parks.

BABI YAR MEMORIAL PARK

10451 E. Yale Ave., Denver, CO 80231

Created in 1982, this 27-acre park commemorates the victims of the 1941–1943 Nazi massacre of Ukrainian Jews and others in Kiev. Within the park is a pathway configured as the Star of David, as well as an amphitheater, a linden tree grove and a ravine. Each area of the park was symbolically and purposely designed.

tclf.org/landscapes/babi-yar-park

CENTRAL PARK

8801 Martin Luther King Jr. Blvd., Denver, CO 80238

When Stapleton International Airport closed in 1995, this 80-acre park and surrounding neighborhood began to be developed. The park contains many paths, fields for team sports, water for boating, hills for sledding, an amphitheater and a Dr. Seuss-inspired playground. Park boundaries are Central Park Boulevard to the west, Martin Luther King Jr. Boulevard to the south, East 33rd Avenue to the north and Dayton Street to the east.

uncovercolorado.com/public-parks/central-park

CHEESMAN PARK

1599 E. 8th St., Denver, CO 80206

Formerly Mount Prospect Cemetery (also known as Denver City Cemetery), this 81-acre land was converted to a park in 1907. Most bodies were moved from the cemetery but some remain below the lawns today. The Cheesman Memorial Pavilion was constructed in 1910. Today, LGBTQ events are often held there, as well as occasional movie nights in the summertime. The park is located between Humboldt Street on the west, Race Street and Denver Botanic Gardens on the east, 13th Avenue on the north and 8th Avenue on the south.

uncovercolorado.com/public-parks/cheesman-park

CITY PARK

1700 N. York St, Denver, CO 80205

This 330-acre park was established in 1880. Within the park are the Denver Museum of Nature and Science and the Denver Zoo. The park also includes two lakes, sports fields, tennis courts, playgrounds and many picnic areas. Festivals and concerts often occur there in the summertime. The park's boundaries are York Street to the west, 17th Avenue to the south, Colorado Boulevard to the east and 23rd Avenue to the north.

uncovercolorado.com/public-parks/city-park

CIVIC CENTER PARK

101 W. 14th Ave. Pkwy., Denver, CO 80202

The 33-acre park opened in 1919. Within the park, you will find a fountain, statues, gardens, a Greek amphitheater, a war memorial and Voorhies Memorial Seal Pond. Civic Center Park holds many festivals, concerts, protests, celebrations, speeches and parades. Many homeless people gather there, as well. In 2008, democratic presidential nominee Barack Obama gave a speech there, and in 2016, Denver Broncos football fans celebrated a Super Bowl win, filling the park with orange shirts and cheers of victory. Favorite yearly festivals include the end of the St. Patrick's Day parade, Cinco de Mayo, People's Fair, Taste of Colorado and many more. Bannock Street borders the park on the west, Broadway on the east, Colfax Avenue on the north and 14th Avenue on the south.

uncovercolorado.com/public-parks/civic-center-park

CONFLUENCE PARK

2250 15th St., Denver, CO 80202

This urban park includes trails, water overlooks, kayak runs, benches and bridges. It is located at the confluence of the South Platte River and Cherry Creek.

uncovercolorado.com/public-parks/
confluence-park-denver

CURTIS PARK

900 32nd St., Denver, CO 80205

This is Denver's first public park, developed in 1868. Mestizo, meaning a mix of cultures and ethnicities, was added to the name in 1987 to reflect the diversity of the community.

denver.org/listing/mestizo-curtis-park/6825

DENVER BOTANIC GARDENS

1007 York St., Denver, CO 80206

This 23-acre park, one of the top five botanic gardens in the nation, was created in 1951. It contains a conservatory, a sunken amphitheater and a variety of themed gardens. This beautiful park sits on top of what used to be Prospect Hill Cemetery. Made entirely of concrete and Plexiglas, the Boettcher Memorial Tropical Conservatory opened in 1966.

botanicgardens.org

DENVER ZOO
2300 Steele St., Denver, CO 80205

The Denver Zoo was founded in 1896. It covers 80 acres and is within Denver City Park. An orphaned black bear cub was its first resident. Bear Mountain was created so that the bear had a more natural habitat than a cage. Over time, other naturalistic enclosures were added, such as Predator Ridge, North Shores, Tropical Discovery, Primate Panorama, and the Toyota Elephant Passage.

denverzoo.org

FOUR MILE HISTORIC PARK
715 S. Forest St., Denver, CO 80246

The City of Denver acquired the house and 12 acres of land in 1975 and opened it as a museum in 1978. This is the site of Denver's oldest house, built in 1859. It was the last stagecoach stop along Smoky Hill Trail before Denver. After railroads replaced stagecoaches, it became a working farm in the 1870s. The park contains a museum, gardens, antique farm equipment and animals.

fourmilepark.org

HUNGARIAN FREEDOM PARK

901 E. 1st Ave., Denver, CO 80218

This small, 3-acre triangular park built on a city dump was previously called Arlington Park. It was developed in 1925. The name of the park was changed to commemorate the 1956 revolt of Hungarians against Soviet oppression. The Hungarian Freedom Monument was installed in the park in 1968.

tclf.org/landscapes/hungarian-freedom-park

OBSERVATORY PARK

2930 E. Iliff Ave., Denver, CO 80210

This neighborhood park houses the Chamberlin Observatory. The building was constructed in 1891 and the first telescope was used there in 1893. The Observatory is operated by the University of Denver.

en.wikipedia.org/wiki/Chamberlin_Observatory

RED ROCKS PARK AND AMPHITHEATRE

18300 W. Alameda Pkwy., Morrison, CO 80465

In 1928, the City of Denver purchased this area and began construction of the open-air amphitheater in 1936. Ever since opening to the public in 1941, many notable performances have been held there, including The Beatles, Johnny Cash, Jimi Hendrix, Jethro Tull, Bob Dylan, U2 and many more. Easter Sunrise Services and Yoga On the Rocks events are held there, weather permitting. In 1973, Red Rocks was designated an official Denver landmark. The Colorado Music Hall of Fame opened inside of the Trading Post in 2015.

redrocksonline.com

SLOAN'S LAKE PARK

1700 N. Sheridan Blvd., Denver, CO 80212

This 290-acre park, including the 177-acre lake, is the second largest in the city. Features of the park include water sports, tennis and basketball courts, grassy areas, soccer fields and a paved path around the lake. The park boundaries are Sheridan Boulevard to the west, 17th Avenue to the south, Raleigh Street to the east and 26th Avenue to the north.

uncovercolorado.com/public-parks/sloans-lake-park

WASHINGTON PARK

S. Downing St. and E. Louisiana Ave., Denver, CO 80210

This 165-acre park was developed in 1899. The park includes two lakes, a boathouse and other historic buildings, tennis courts, flower gardens, a recreation center and large lawn. The park is long and rectangular. It is bordered by Virginia Avenue on the north, Downing Street on the west, Louisiana Avenue on the south and Franklin Street on the east.

uncovercolorado.com/public-parks/washington-park

WATER

RIVERS, CREEKS, CANALS AND LAKES

Although water is not plentiful in Denver, enjoy exploring its largest lakes and waterways.

CHERRY CREEK

This creek begins in El Paso County south of Denver, winds through Castlewood Canyon and into Denver, passing through Parker, Aurora and Centennial along the way. It connects to South Platte at Confluence Park. It is approximately 48 miles in length. A search for gold in 1858 at this confluence was part of the beginning of what later became Denver City. It was named "Cherry" Creek because of chokecherry bushes along its banks.

en.wikipedia.org/wiki/Cherry_Creek_(Colorado)

CLEAR CREEK

A tributary of South Platte, it begins at the Continental Divide near Loveland Pass and runs down Clear Creek Canyon. It emerges on the eastern plains at Golden, running through Coors Brewery. It goes through Lakewood and Wheat Ridge, roughly running along Interstate 76. It passes under Interstate 25 in the junction of I-70 and Highway 36 (Boulder Turnpike), before finally joining the South Platte in southeast Thornton. It is approximately 66 miles long.

en.wikipedia.org/wiki/Clear_Creek_(Colorado)

HIGH LINE CANAL

At 71 miles long, it meanders through Denver alongside a wonderful path for bikers and walkers. This man-made canal was created for irrigation for farmers and ranchers in 1883. It begins near Waterton Canyon in Littleton and runs to Aurora near Spring Hill Golf Course. It still services some irrigation needs but has mostly changed its purpose to recreational. In 1978, it was designated as a National Recreation Trail.

highlinecanal.org

SLOAN'S LAKE

This lake is located west of downtown Denver. Thomas Sloan was a homesteader and dug a well in this area, hitting an aquifer that caused flooding of over 200 acres around 1862. The lake opened to the public in 1881. Today, the lake is 177 acres and has a park surrounding it for recreation and enjoyment.

uncovercolorado.com/public-parks/sloans-lake-park

SOUTH PLATTE RIVER

This river originates in Park County near Fairplay. When it reaches Littleton, it fills Chatfield Reservoir before moving on to Denver. It eventually joins the North Platte in western Nebraska to form the Platte River. It is 439 miles long. Platte means flat in French.

en.wikipedia.org/wiki/South_Platte_River

FURTHER EXPLORATION

More About Parks

denvergov.org/content/denvergov/en/denver-parks-and-recreation/parks.html

denver.org/things-to-do/sports-recreation/denver-parks

uncovercolorado.com/public-parks/

Books for Walking Tours and Trails

denverbyfoot.com

mindysink.com/walking-denver-2nd-edition

City Beautiful Movement

coloradoencyclopedia.org/article/city-beautiful-movement-denver

coloradovirtuallibrary.org/digital-colorado/colorado-histories/20th-century/robert-speer-denvers-city-beautiful-mayor/

PEOPLE

Many remarkable women and men have enhanced Denver's history and the present. It is challenging to know when to stop adding names, so this is a sampling of notable people with resources for further exploration at the end of the list.

MARGARET "MOLLY" BROWN

1867–1932

Margaret was known posthumously as "The Unsinkable Molly Brown" because she survived the 1912 sinking of the Titanic. Her legacy is philanthropic. She advocated for the rights of workers and women, education and literacy for children, preservation and other causes of social reform. She was inducted into the Colorado Women's Hall of Fame in 1985.

mollybrown.org/about-molly-brown

ELIZABETH "LIBBY" BYERS

1834–1920

Elizabeth Byers was a social reformer focusing on the poor and was instrumental in establishing and supporting Denver's early charitable organizations, schools and churches. Her husband was William Byers

(1831–1903). He founded the *Rocky Mountain News*, Denver's first newspaper.

coloradoencyclopedia.org/article/elizabeth-byers

DANA CRAWFORD

1931–

Crawford is a preservationist who saved the 1400 block of Larimer Street from demolition and created the treasure of Larimer Square that we enjoy today. She also brought the loft lifestyle to Denver. The first loft in Denver opened

in 1990 with the Edbrooke building at 1450 Wynkoop Street. She continues to be involved in various preservation projects and was inducted to the Colorado Women's Hall of Fame for "Saving the Soul of Denver."

danacrawford.net/home.html

BARNEY LANCELOT FORD

1822–1902

Ford escaped slavery via the Underground Railroad and became a civil rights pioneer who fought Colorado statehood until African Americans gained the right to vote. He built the

Inter-Ocean Hotel and People's Restaurant in Denver. Ford is a member of the Colorado Black Hall of Fame and Colorado Business Hall of Fame. He has a stained-glass portrait in the

House Chamber of the State Capitol building. One of his homes in Breckenridge is a museum and open for tours. He is buried in Riverside Cemetery in Commerce City.

coloradoencyclopedia.org/article/barney-ford

breckheritage.com/barney-ford-victorian-home

DR. JUSTINA L. FORD

1871–1952

Ford was the first licensed African American female doctor in Denver. She moved to Denver in 1902 and practiced obstetrics and gynecology, as well as pediatrics, from her home at 2335 Arapahoe Street. She also made house calls. She practiced for fifty years and treated anyone, regardless of race or ability to pay. Her home moved from Arapahoe Street to 3091 California Street and became the home of the Black American West Museum.

coloradovirtuallibrary.org/digital-colo-rado/colorado-histories/20th-century/justina-ford-denvers-first-female-african-american-doctor/

RODOLFO "CORKY" GONZALES

1928–2005

Gonzales was a Chicano boxer as well as a poet, political organizer and activist. He established the Crusade for Justice and wrote the poem "Yo Soy Joaquin" (I Am Joaquin). The poem described his community's struggle for social and economic justice and the evolution of Chicano culture.

history.denverlibrary.org/rodolfo-corky-gonzales

EMILY GRIFFITH

1868–1947

Emily Griffith was an educator and founded the Opportunity School in Denver in 1916. She believed that immigrant children and their parents needed to learn English and job skills. It was a unique school, which offered job training and education "For All Those Who

Wish To Learn." Griffith was a proponent that education was the only way to lift people from poverty. Emily Griffith Opportunity School, later called Technical College and High School, is located at 1860 Lincoln Street, Denver, CO 80203. When Emily retired, she moved to Pinecliffe, Colorado, to live with her sister. In 1947, she and her sister were murdered, and to this day, the crime was never solved.

history.denverlibrary.org/colorado-biographies/
emily-griffith-1868-1947

FRANCES WISEBART JACOB

1843–1892

Jacob initially focused on the Jewish community, organizing and becoming president of the Hebrew Ladies' Relief Society in 1872. She expanded her reach to include anyone suffering from poverty and illness by establishing the Denver Women's Relief Society in 1874. Jacob founded the first free kindergarten in Denver. She continued her work by creating Charity Organization Society, which later became United Way. Before her death she worked to bring a sanatorium to Denver to help those with tuberculous. She became known as Denver's "mother of charities." She was inducted into the Colorado Women's Hall of Fame in 1985.

jwa.org/encyclopedia/article/jacobs-frances-wisebart

coloradovirtuallibrary.org/digital-col-
orado/colorado-histories/beginnings/
frances-wisebart-jacobs-health-care-activist

FEDERICO PEÑA

1947–

Peña was an attorney and the first Latino mayor of Denver, serving from 1983–1991. He was also the United States Secretary of Transportation (1993–1997) and the United States Secretary of Energy (1997–1998). Peña Boulevard was named after him and connects Denver International Airport to Interstate 70. Peña led the effort to build the airport and bring major league baseball to Denver. He resurrected the City Beautiful Movement by restoring parks and parkways and preserving historic buildings. He was also instrumental in facilitating an addition to the Central Library and a new convention center.

coloradovirtuallibrary.org/digital-colo-
rado/colorado-histories/20th-century/
federico-pena-mayor-of-denver

"DADDY" BRUCE RANDOLPH

1900–1994

Randolph was known as a community advocate, restaurateur and Colorado Black Hall of Fame Inductee. Daddy Bruce's Bar-B-Que restaurant opened in 1963 at the corner of Gilpin Street and East 34th Avenue. Daddy Bruce began a tradition on Thanksgiving Day by taking a truck full of ribs to City Park and feeding the hungry. Bruce Randolph Avenue was named on the section of 34th Avenue from Downing to Dahlia, and in 2008, Bruce Randolph School opened to grades six to twelve in his honor.

history.denverlibrary.org/news/
exhbit-spirit-daddy-bruce-randolph

CHIEF LITTLE RAVEN

1810–1889

Little Raven was a Chief of Southern Arapaho who welcomed and offered hospitality to white prospectors. He desired a peaceful co-existence with whites. He also negotiated peace between tribes and secured rights for the Cheyenne-Arapaho Reservation. He survived the Sand Creek Massacre in 1864. Little Raven Street along Riverfront Park between 15th and 20th Streets is named after him.

coloradovirtuallibrary.org/digital-col-orado/colorado-histories/beginnings/chief-little-raven-peacemaker

en.wikipedia.org/wiki/Sand_Creek_massacre

ROBERT WALTER SPEER

1855–1918

Speer came to Colorado to recover from tuberculous. His first job in Denver was at the Daniels and Fisher Department Store. He then became Denver's city clerk and later the postmaster, as he moved into politics. He was first elected mayor of Denver in 1904 and was instrumental in bringing the "City Beautiful" era to Denver. He died of influenza during the epidemic of 1918.

coloradovirtuallibrary.org/digital-colo-rado/colorado-histories/20th-century/robert-speer-denvers-city-beautiful-mayor

WELLINGTON WEBB

1941–

Webb served in the Colorado House of Representatives and was the first African American mayor of Denver (1991–2003). He served three terms as mayor of Denver. His four areas of focus were parks and open space, public safety, economic development and children. He was instrumental in the South Platte River Corridor Project, which encompassed commercial and residential redevelopment and reclamation of parkland along the river. The Wellington E. Webb Municipal Office Building at 201 W. Colfax Avenue, Denver, CO 80202 was completed in 2002 and was named in honor of Webb.

en.wikipedia.org/wiki/Wellington_Webb

FURTHER EXPLORATION

Notable Women

coloradoencyclopedia.org/person/women

Center for Colorado Women's History

historycolorado.org/center-colorado-womens-history

Colorado Women's Hall of Fame

en.wikipedia.org/wiki/Colorado_Women%27s_Hall_of_Fame

Notable Coloradans

historycolorado.org/biographies-notable-coloradans

Lists of People from Denver in Multiple Categories

en.wikipedia.org/wiki/List_of_people_from_Denver

PUBLIC ART

Art lovers can enjoy outdoor art throughout the city in parks and near landmark buildings. Enjoy an ever-growing list of a few of the most infamous statues and art displays in Denver.

SCULPTURES

ART MUSEUM AND CENTRAL LIBRARY
100 W. 14th Ave. Pkwy., Denver, CO 80204

Denver Monoliths
The artist is Beverly Pepper. The sculpture was installed in 2006. The two massive vertical elements are 42 feet tall and 31 feet tall and are made of composite cementitious material.

For Jennifer
The artist is Joel Shapiro, who created the sculpture in memory of Jennifer Moulton. This 32-foot-tall aluminum work in blue is simple yet dynamic.

Pilgrimage

Artist Zhang Huan created this lifesize granite sculpture of himself as a naked man face down. Zhang performed the feat of lying naked and face down for ten minutes on a public street on a block of ice placed on a traditional Chinese bed. Zhang created the sculpture to describe his experience coming to America and his fear of New York City. It was moved to its current location in 2011.

Scottish Angus Cow and Calf

The artist is Dan Ostermiller and the sculpture was installed in 2001. The bronze animals are three times lifesize at 38 by 22 feet and the artwork weighs about 5 tons.

The Big Sweep

The artists are Claes Oldenburg and Coosje Van Bruggen. The structure was completed in 2006. This 35-foot-tall broom and dustpan are made primarily of aluminum and steel. It weighs over 2,000 pounds.

The Yearling

The artist is Donald Lipski, and the sculpture was completed in 1998. This 21-foot-tall sculpture is a lifesize horse on an enormous red chair. The chair is made of steel, and the painted pinto pony is made of fiberglass.

ARTICULATED WALL

625 S. Broadway,
Denver, CO 80209

The artist is Herbert Bayer, and the sculpture was installed in 1985. This yellow sculpture is 85 feet tall and is made of concrete.

CITY PARK
Denver, CO 80205

Martin Luther King Jr. Statue and Memorial

This statue was created by Edward Joseph (Ed) Dwight Jr. The memorial was installed in 2002 in the south part of City Park off 17th Avenue. It also features Frederick Douglass, Mohandas 'Mahatma' Gandhi, Rosa Parks and Sojourner Truth, and four tablets representing Slavery, Struggle, Justice and Living the Dream.

Thatcher Memorial Fountain

This memorial was created by Lorado Zadok and dedicated in 1918. It is located in City Park Esplanade. The central figure is surrounded by groups depicting loyalty, love and learning.

CIVIC CENTER PARK

Civic Center Park, Denver, CO 80202

Bronco Buster

Created by Alexander Phimister Proctor and installed in 1920.

On the War Trail

Created by Alexander Phimister Proctor and installed in 1922.

Pioneer Fountain

Created by Frederick William MacMonnies and opened in 1911. Also known as Pioneer Monument.

Additional Sculptures and Monuments

Many sculptures were vandalized and removed in 2020, so the area of Civic Center Park is in transition.

COLORADO CONVENTION CENTER

700 14tsh St., Denver, CO 80202

I See What You Mean / Blue Bear

This statue was created by Lawrence Argent. Rising to 40 feet tall and looking in on the Convention Center, it is also known as the Big Blue Bear.

DENVER INTERNATIONAL AIRPORT

8500 Peña Blvd., Denver, CO 80249

DIA has many permanent and temporary exhibits. The main terminal roof is designed to reflect snow-capped mountains and evoke images of Native American teepees.

Blue Mustang

Located at Denver International Airport in the median of Peña Boulevard, this 32-foot-tall and 9,000-pound blue mustang with red eyes fell on its creator, Luis A. Jiménez Jr., killing him. The sculpture was unveiled in 2008 and is nicknamed Blucifer.

DENVER PERFORMING ARTS COMPLEX

1101 13th St., Denver, CO 80204

Dancers

Located in the Denver Performing Arts Sculpture Park, this sculpture was created by Jonathan Borofsky and installed in 2003. The steel and fiberglass dancers stand 60 feet tall. Music plays from a speaker and visitors are encouraged to dance too.

Man and Woman

Located in the Denver
Performing Arts Galleria, this
art was created by Fernando
Botero. The portly bronze
figures were installed in 1998
to welcome theatergoers.

EAST 2 WEST
SOURCE POINT

201 W. Colfax Ave.,
Denver, CO 80202

Located in front of the
Wellington E. Webb Municipal
Building, this granite sculpture
includes two faces and a golden
plumb bob. It was created in
2003 by Larry Kirkland. It is

surrounded by historical maps of Denver, and it is set exactly
on the lines of latitude and longitude which define Denver's
location on the globe. The two faces represent the Greek God
Janus, who looks toward the future and the past. The plumb
bob is a hand tool used to determine if a vertical surface is true,
symbolizing the ideal that our civic government should be based
upon truth.

HUNGARIAN FREEDOM MONUMENT

901 E. 1st Ave., Denver, CO 80218

Artists Zoltan and Stephen Popovitis created this bronze figure showing a man's desperate attempt to break through a symbolic curtain, but he is restrained by it. The artists wished to express the human aspiration for liberty and the will to survive. The monument was installed in Hungarian Freedom Park in 1968.

NATIONAL VELVET

2415 16th St., Denver, CO 80202

Created by artist John McEnroe, this obelisk was installed in 2008 and is located on the Highland Pedestrian Bridge. It stands 20 feet tall and is made of fiberglass, aluminum, paint and resin.

MURALS

ART DISTRICT OF SANTA FE

This district features murals as well as museums, theaters and the Center for Visual Arts. First Friday events are held each month with artists in studios and galleries, music, food trucks and more.

denver.org/about-denver/neighborhood-guides/artdistrict-on-santa-fe

denversartdistrict.org/first-friday

RINO ARTS DISTRICT

The largest collection of murals in Denver are located in River North Arts District along the Larimer Street corridor. Enjoy galleries and markets along with craft beer, wine and spirits. Crush Walls (Creative Rituals Under Social

Harmony) is a yearly event with artists creating new open-air murals and galleries.

denver.org/about-denver/neighborhood-guides/
river-north-art-district

crushwalls.org

FURTHER EXPLORATION

Public Art Displays
denverpublicart.org

denver.org/things-to-do/denver-arts-culture/public-art

en.wikipedia.org/wiki/List_of_public_art_in_Denver

Denver International Airport Displays
flydenver.com/art

SCHOOLS

Denver has many schools of historical significance. Some of the oldest and most well-known schools are included here as a starting point to understand Denver's upper grades, colleges and universities.

HIGH SCHOOLS

The original four high schools in Denver all had the word "Side" in them: East Side, West Side, North Side and South Side high schools. In the 1920s, "Side" was officially dropped from their names.

East High School
1600 City Park Esplanade,
Denver, CO 80206

Denver's first high school was built in 1924. It opened in 1875 and was originally located at 19th and Stout Streets. The architect, George Hebard Williamson, was a graduate of "Old East." He designed the clock tower after Independence Hall in Philadelphia.

East High School was the first school involved in the City Beautiful Movement. Mayor Speer wanted each high school to border a park. As a result, East High School was moved to City Park in 1922. Their mascot is the Angels.

east.dpsk12.org

North High School

2960 Speer Blvd.,
Denver, CO 80211

Originally in the separate
town of Highland, this
school graduated its first class in 1886. In 1896, the town
of Highland was incorporated into the city of Denver. The
current building, located at Speer Blvd., was built in 1911
bordering Highland Park. Their mascot is the Vikings.

north.dpsk12.org

South High School

1700 E. Louisiana Ave.,
Denver, CO 80210

Established in 1893, it was
moved to its present location on Louisiana Avenue
in 1926, next to Washington Park. Their mascot is the Ravens,
formerly the Rebels.

denversouth.dpsk12.org

West High School
951 Elati St., Denver, CO 80204

Denver's second high school was organized in 1883. It moved to its current location on Elati Street by Sunken Garden Park in 1926. Their mascot is the Cowboys.

westleadershipacademy.dpsk12.org

Manual High School
1700 E. 28th Ave., Denver, CO 80205

The original building was opened in 1892 as an extension of East High School. Manual Training School taught practical skills such as wood and metal working. Manual was also one of the first schools in Denver to educate African Americans. In 1953, the building was destroyed by a fire, and a new building was built nearby and opened in 1954. "Training" was dropped from the name. The school was closed in 2006, but due to student protests and community outrage over the closure, it was reopened in 2007. Their mascot is the Thunderbolts.

manual.dpsk12.org

COLLEGES AND UNIVERSITIES

UNIVERSITY OF DENVER

2199 S. University Blvd.,
Denver, CO 80208

It was founded in 1864 by John
Evans, former governor of the
Colorado Territory. It was originally called and still legally
named the Colorado Seminary. It was renamed in 1880 as
the University of Denver. Buildings were originally located
downtown but moved to a potato farm south of downtown.
University Hall (built in 1890) is the oldest building on
campus. Their mascot is the Pioneers.

du.edu

METROPOLITAN STATE UNIVERSITY OF DENVER

890 Auraria Pkwy., Denver, CO 80204

Metro State was established in 1965 and is located on the
Auraria Campus. Their mascot is the Roadrunner.

msudenver.edu

UNIVERSITY OF COLORADO DENVER

Auraria Campus

1201 Larimer St., Denver, CO 80204

Established in 1912. Their mascot is the Lynx.

ucdenver.edu

Anschutz Medical Campus

1635 Aurora Ct., Aurora, CO 80045

Founded in 2006 and opened in 2007. Contains six science- and health-related schools and colleges.

cuanschutz.edu

COMMUNITY COLLEGE OF DENVER

800 Curtis St., Denver, CO 80204

Established in 1967 and located on the Auraria Campus. Their mascot is the Hawk.

ccd.edu

LORETTO HEIGHTS CAMPUS

3001 S. Federal Blvd., Denver, CO 80236

This campus has been home to many schools and is currently in transition. In 1886, Loretto Heights Academy was founded as a Catholic girls' high school. Over the years, the school became a college and a university and added buildings to the campus. The future of the campus was not determined at the time of publication of this book.

historicdenver.org/loretto-heights-whats-next

REGIS UNIVERSITY

3333 Regis Blvd., Denver, CO 80221

As a private Jesuit university, Regis was founded in 1877. Its mascot is the Rangers.

regis.edu

FURTHER EXPLORATION

History of Directional High Schools

history.denverlibrary.org/news/
north-south-east-west-denvers-iconic-public-high-schools

SPORTS, STADIUMS AND RODEOS

Sports are hugely popular in Denver, and the city currently has five professional sports teams.

FOOTBALL: DENVER BRONCOS

Founded in 1960. Mascot: "Thunder," a purebred Arabian gelding

denverbroncos.com

BASKETBALL: DENVER NUGGETS

Founded in 1967. Mascot: "Rocky," a mountain lion

nba.com/nuggets

BASEBALL: COLORADO ROCKIES

Founded in 1993. Mascot: "Dinger," a dinosaur

mlb.com/rockies

HOCKEY: COLORADO AVALANCHE

Founded in 1995. Mascot: "Bernie," a St. Bernard

nhl.com/avalanche

SOCCER: COLORADO RAPIDS

Founded in 1996. Mascot: "Rapid Man," a blue-faced man

coloradorapids.com

The Broncos won the Super Bowl in 1997, 1998 and 2015.

The Avalanche won the Stanley Cup in 1996 and 2001.

The Rapids won the MLS (Major League Soccer) Cup in 2010.

ADDITIONAL PROFESSIONAL TEAMS:

LACROSSE: COLORADO MAMMOTH
Founded in 2003. Mascot: "Wooly," a mammoth

coloradomammoth.com

DENVER OUTLAWS
Founded in 2006. Mascot: "Stix," a raccoon

outlaws.majorleaguelacrosse.com

STADIUMS

BALL ARENA, FORMERLY PEPSI CENTER

1000 Chopper Cir., Denver, CO 80204

Capacity: 20,000

Opened in 1999, this is the home court/rink/field for the Denver Nuggets, the Colorado Avalanche and the Colorado Mammoth teams. It is also a concert venue and was involved in the 2008 Democratic National Convention.

ballarena.com

COORS FIELD

2001 Blake St., Denver, CO 80205

Capacity: 50,398

Opened in 1995, this is the home field for the Colorado Rockies baseball team. During construction, excavators discovered dinosaur fossils. Installed in 1995 at the Wynkoop entrance, The Evolution of the Ball is a ceramic and steel sculpture designed by Lonnie Hanzon.

mlb.com/rockies/ballpark

DICK'S SPORTING GOODS PARK

6000 Victory Way, Commerce City, CO 80022

Capacity: 18,061 (soccer); 27,000 (concert)

Opened in 2007, this is the home field of the Colorado Rapids soccer team. It has also served as a popular music venue.

dickssportinggoodspark.com

EMPOWER FIELD AT MILE HIGH, FORMERLY INVESCO FIELD AND SPORTS AUTHORITY FIELD

1701 Bryant St., Denver, CO 80204

Capacity: 76,125

Opened in 2001, this is the home stadium for the Denver Broncos football team. It has also held many big-name concerts such as Garth Brooks in 2019, which had a crowd of 84,000, made possible by additional seating on the field.

President Obama gave his acceptance speech at the 2008 Democratic National Convention in the stadium. Above the south stands, you can find a 27-foot-tall bucking bronco named Bucky.

denverbroncos.com

INFINITY PARK
950 S. Birch St., Glendale, CO 80246

Capacity: 5,000

Opened in 2007, it is a premier rugby stadium.

infinityparkatglendale.com

OTHER SPORTS VENUES

CITY PARK GOLF COURSE
3181 E. 23rd Ave., Denver, CO 80205

Opened in 1913, it has a recently redesigned 18-hole course.

cityofdenvergolf.com/city_park

DENVER ATHLETIC CLUB

1325 Glenarm Pl., Denver, CO 80204

Founded in 1884, the social and athletic club moved to its current location in 1890 on Glenarm Place.

denverathleticclub.cc

DENVER COUNTRY CLUB

1700 E. 1st Ave., Denver, CO 80218

Founded in 1887, this is the oldest country club west of the Mississippi River. It was originally centered on horseracing but expanded to tennis, polo, golf and other sports.

denvercc.net

DENVER TURNVEREIN

1570 N. Clarkson St., Denver, CO 80218

Built in 1921, the building was used for German culture, exercise and a social club. It is currently a dance club with a beautiful dance floor and offers lessons almost every night of the week.

denverturnverein.com

OVERLAND COUNTRY CLUB, FORMERLY DENVER COUNTRY CLUB

1801 S. Huron St., Denver, CO 80223

Opened in 1895, this 18-hole course is the oldest golf course in Denver and is the oldest operating course west of the

Mississippi River. The area also used to include a racetrack, first for horses and later for autos.

cityofdenvergolf.com/overland_park

RODEOS

THE NATIONAL WESTERN STOCK SHOW
4655 Humboldt St., Denver, CO 80216

This event has been held in Denver every January since 1906, and the first rodeo was held in 1931. Its original purpose was to demonstrate better breeding and feeding techniques to stockmen. It is governed by the National Western Stock Show

Association and its mission is: "To preserve the western life-style by providing a showcase for the agricultural industry through emphasis on education, genetic development, innovative technology and offering the world's largest agricultural marketing opportunities."

You can enjoy horse shows and exhibits, rodeos, livestock exhibits and trade shows. Each year the event kicks off with a parade downtown from Union Station down 17th Street, in which cowboys (both male and female) herd more than forty Longhorn cattle.

nationalwestern.com

AFRICAN AMERICAN RODEO

The first rodeo was held in Denver in 1947. Smokey Lornes sponsored the rodeo to help Black cowboys get started and prove their worth. The National Western's MLK Jr. Rodeo was founded by Lu Vason and launched in 2006. According to *Smithsonian Magazine*, one in four American cowboys were Black.

smithsonianmag.com/history/lesser-known-history-african-american-cowboys-180962144

MEXICAN RODEO EXTRAVAGANZA

First held in 1994, this rodeo is part of the National Western Stock Show. It features performances of dancers, singers, horse dancing, trick riding, bullfighting minus the bloodshed, and much more. It celebrates the Mexican cowboy, a charro, and the heritage and culture of the Mexican people.

STORES AND SHOPPING

The hub of retail and shopping started downtown. In the 1950s, shopping malls began to be built in the suburbs of most cities. In the following decades as more and more outlying malls were built, fewer people shopped at downtown department stores, and it became difficult for those large stores to compete and stay in business. Today, Denver still has clusters of shopping areas available downtown. This section honors great stores that are now closed and current ones that offer shopping opportunities.

LARIMER SQUARE

Larimer Street was the original Main Street in Denver. Thanks to preservation work in the 1970s, the one block of Larimer from 14th to 15th streets was saved from demolition and revitalized. It is now referred to as Larimer Square and is filled with retail, restaurants and some residential lofts. Outdoor dining, festivals and events are often held in this gem of a block.

larimersquare.com

16TH STREET MALL

In the 1880s and 1890s, 16th Street overtook Larimer as Denver's main street. Many retail stores began to be built along 16th Street. In 1980, construction began for a pedestrian corridor (16th Street Mall), and it opened in 1982. Many department stores used to be along this street. Most large stores have closed or been repurposed, but many small stores remain. The mall runs 1.25 miles long from Wewatta Street at Union Station to the intersection of 16th Avenue and Broadway (Civic Center Station).

the16thstreetmall.com

DANIELS AND FISHER TOWER AND STORE

1601 Arapahoe St., Denver, CO 80202

Merchant William B. Daniels came to Denver in 1864 and established a dry goods business. He became a business partner with William Garrett Fisher in 1872. The company became quite successful in the 1890s as the largest retailer in the state.

The Daniels and Fisher department store opened in 1910 at 1101 16th Street. The tower, which still remains today, was erected in 1911. The tower was supposed to resemble Saint Mark's in Venice, Italy. The twenty-story clock tower was placed on the National Register of Historic

Places in 1969. The adjoining store was demolished in 1971. The tower includes a 2½-ton bell and observation deck at the top with office and residential space on the twenty floors below. In the basement is an entertainment venue called Lannie's Clocktower Cabaret.

The store closed in 1957 when it merged with the May Company. The new May-D&F store opened further up 16th Street. In 1987, May D&F absorbed three stores of The Denver Dry Goods Company. It merged with Foley's in 1993 and was then absorbed by Macy's in 2005. The downtown location at 350 16th Street closed in 1993 and was demolished in 1994, later becoming a Hilton Hotel.

DENVER DRY GOODS COMPANY

702 16th St., Denver, CO 80202

"The Denver" was established in 1879 by Michael J. McNamara and L.H. Flanders as M.J. McNamara & Company. The original downtown location was built in 1889 and converted to lofts in 1994. The store enjoyed expansion to additional suburb locations but eventually folded in 1987. Many Colorado residents fondly recall the store motto, "Where Colorado Shops With Confidence."

JOSLINS DRY GOODS COMPANY / JOSLINS DEPARTMENT STORE

934 16th St., Denver, CO 80202

Jay Joslin founded this store in 1873. The 16th Street location was built in 1887. It was eventually converted to Dillards and went defunct in 1998. The building currently houses the Courtyard by Marriott hotel.

NEUSTETERS DEPARTMENT STORE

720 16th St., Denver, CO 80202

Founded by Max David Neusteter, this store opened in 1924 in a building that was built in 1894. This store expanded to suburbs and the last store, at the Cherry Creek Mall, closed in 1986. The original building was converted to lofts and condominiums and ground-floor retail.

SAKURA SQUARE

1255 19th St., Denver, CO 80202

This collection of retail and restaurants opened in 1973. The square celebrates Japanese American history and culture and includes three statues featuring Ralph Carr, Attorney Minoru Yasui and Reverend Yoshitaka Tamai, notable in Colorado's history of Japanese Americans.

sakurasquare.com

CHERRY CREEK SHOPPING CENTER

3000 E. 1st Ave., Denver, CO 80206

This complex was originally completed in 1953 and renovated in 1990. The land under the mall was a reclamation project. Before it was a shopping center, sand was mined from a large pit. When the area was mined out, it became a landfill. Thus, this shopping center is built atop a trash dump.

shopcherrycreek.com

FURTHER EXPLORATION

Daniels and Fisher Tower

coloradoencyclopedia.org/article/daniels-and-fisher-tower

Clock Tower Events and Tours

clocktowerevents.com/tours.html

The Denver Department Store

thedepartmentstoremuseum.org/2010/06/denver-denver-colorado.html

Joslins

thedepartmentstoremuseum.org/2012/01/joslins-denver-colorado.html

Neusteters

history.denverlibrary.org/news/neusteters

Lost Department Stores of Denver

arcadiapublishing.com/Products/9781467138406

STREETS, INTERSTATES AND TRANSPORTATION

STREETS

The streets of Denver are laid out on two grids. One is directional and the other is diagonal. The oldest part of downtown Denver, including Auraria and Five Points, has its streets on a diagonal grid. As you move outward from there and into the surrounding suburbs, the streets are on a directional grid. The reason the inner city and original portion of Denver streets are diagonal is because Auraria platted streets paralleling Cherry Creek, and Denver aligned with the South Platte. In 1864, the directional grid was added toward the east and south for the central downtown area.

Some roads, such as Leetsdale Drive and South Santa Fe Drive, do not stay directional, as they were county roads and routes of early settlers.

Eventually, city leaders decided that streets would run north-south, and avenues, places and drives would run east-west. Streets use the 100s numbering system, with courts as mid-100s. Ways begin north-south and then curve to intersect with another north-south route. Boulevards, roads and parkways were major arterials.

Gradually in the late 1800s, a modern decimal grid was developed. For example, 1st Street is the 100 block. In the directional grid part of the city, even-number addresses are on the east side of streets and south side of avenues. Odd numbers are on the west side of streets and on the north side of avenues. Broadway (north-south) and Ellsworth Avenue (east-west) form axes. Thereby streets south of Ellsworth insert a "South" into their names and those north of it insert a "North" for clarity of direction. Avenues east of Broadway add "East" to their official address and those west of it add "West."

Some parts of town have streets in alphabetical order. Denver also has numbered streets, currently extending into the 100s. Another area has streets with famous universities.

BROADWAY

Denver's major north-south artery, Broadway is uninterrupted throughout the city for approximately 20 miles. As it goes south, it passes through old downtown Englewood and just east of old downtown Littleton. After passing County Line Road, it enters Highlands Ranch and begins to curve left and right and eventually ends at approximately Wildcat Reserve Parkway.

Originally, this street had Denver Tramway Company trolleys taking passengers to the suburbs of Capitol Hill, Baker and Washington Parks. South Broadway hosts Antique Row (approximately a hundred antique stores in eighteen blocks) and the Mayan Theatre.

COLFAX AVENUE

Denver's most infamous street is Colfax Avenue (which is also 15th Avenue), and it runs east-west. It is 26 miles in length and first appeared on maps in 1868. The street was named after Schuyler Colfax, a 19th century politician. It is also Highway 40, one of two principle highways serving Denver before interstate development. Colfax has much history and many landmarks along it. Movies have been filmed on Colfax. It was designated as a Colorado Heritage Corridor in the late 1990s. Notable restaurants, large mansions, schools, churches, the Mint and many other recognizable places have a Colfax address. In the 1970s, the street was dubbed the "longest, wickedest street in America," but there is a debate if *Playboy Magazine* actually printed that description as claimed. However, Colfax is known as the longest commercial street in the United States.

SANTA FE DRIVE

It is a north-south route that merges with Highway 85. Closer to downtown, the Arts District on Santa Fe Drive hosts more than thirty art galleries and studios. It also includes authentic Mexican culture with the Museo de las Americas and Su Teatro Cultural and Performing Arts Center. The district offers First Friday Art Walks and includes the Colorado Ballet and the Buckhorn Exchange restaurant.

SPEER BOULEVARD

Built in 1906, this boulevard runs from Irving Street in the West Highland neighborhood to Downing Street. It is named for Robert W. Speer, known for bringing the City Beautiful Movement to Denver. He served as mayor from 1904–1912 and 1916–1918. It runs along Cherry Creek and is part of the Denver Park and Parkway System, which includes sixteen parkways and fifteen parks.

INTERSTATES

Five interstates exist in Colorado and run through Denver. Construction of the Valley Highway began in 1948. It started to the north at 52nd Avenue between Acoma and Bannock Streets, and ended to the south at Colorado and Buchtel Boulevards.

In 1956, the Federal-Aid Highway Act, also known as National Interstate and Defense Highways Act, was enacted. One purpose was to defend the US if it came under attack. "In the event of a ground invasion by a foreign power, the US Army would need good highways to be able to transport troops across the country efficiently."

In 1958, the Valley Highway became Interstate 25, but signage did not reflect the change until many years later. Even when the signs eventually changed to reflect the interstate, people often still referred to I-25 as the Valley Highway. Gradually, I-25 extended in both directions. In 1969, it was complete from the Wyoming state line to the north and to Walsenburg to the south for a total of 299 miles. Currently I-25 is a total of 305 miles from the state lines of Wyoming to the north and New Mexico to the south.

Interstate 70 runs 449 miles through Colorado from the state lines of Kansas and Utah. Its construction was mostly started and completed in the sixties and seventies, but the difficult section was Glenwood Canyon, which was not completed until 1992. The Mousetrap is the informal name of the I-70 and I-25 interchange built in 1951. The name "mousetrap" was coined by the long-time airborne radio traffic reporter Don Martin in the 1960s, calling the interchange "a maze that could trap a mouse."

Interstate 76 is 183 miles in length, begins in Arvada, and runs toward Nebraska in a northeast direction. It was created in 1975. I-225 and I-270 are short interstates within Denver at a length of 11 and 5 miles, respectively.

TRANSPORTATION

In 1872, horse-drawn streetcars were the first form of public transportation in Denver. They were run by the Denver Horse Railroad Company. Two horses pulled cars along 2 miles of track from 7th and Larimer Street to 27th and Champa Street. Cable cars with sunken cables, as well as steam and electric cable cars, evolved gradually. Ridership peaked in 1910. The Denver Tramway Company owned the majority of the lines. As automobiles became more prevalent, use of streetcars declined. Buses powered by overhead electrical lines were developed in the 1920s and early 1930s. The last streetcar lines were removed in 1950.

RTD (Regional Transportation District) provides bus and rail service in Denver. The organization began in 1994. Commuter types include bus, commuter rail and light rail.

UNION STATION

1701 Wynkoop St., Denver, CO 80202

This station is a transit hub for Denver. It opened in 1881, although the first train arrived in Denver in 1870. The Denver Pacific line was built to connect Denver to the main line in Wyoming, which was the coast-to-coast route. Originally, there were four rail stations in Denver, which was inconvenient for travelers. Union Station united the four stations. A fire occurred at the station in 1894. The central portion of the building we see today was erected in 1914. A major renovation occurred in 2012 and Union Station now includes restaurants, a hotel, shops and nearby housing.

ART-n-TRANSIT

Thanks to RTD's Art-n-Transit program, you can enjoy an eclectic array of public art pieces at more than forty-five rail stations and bus terminals throughout the metro area.

DENVER INTERNATIONAL AIRPORT (DIA)

The airport was opened in 1995 and is now the hub for both United Airlines and Frontier Airlines and a base for Southwest Airlines. At 33,531 acres (52.4 square miles), it is the largest airport in North America by land area. Runway 16R/34L, with a length of 16,000 feet (3.03 miles), is the longest public-use runway in North America. As of 2019, "DEN" is the 18th busiest airport in the world—the fifth busiest in the US.

FURTHER EXPLORATION

Street Systems of Denver

en.wikipedia.org/wiki/Street_system_of_Denver

Colfax Avenue

colfaxavenue.org

en.wikipedia.org/wiki/Colfax_Avenue

Denver Arts District on Santa Fe

denversartdistrict.org

Speer Boulevard

en.wikipedia.org/wiki/Speer_Boulevard

Interstates

en.wikipedia.org/wiki/Federal_Aid_Highway_Act_of_1956

en.wikipedia.org/wiki/Mousetrap_(Denver)

en.wikipedia.org/wiki/List_of_Interstate_Highways_in_Colorado

Transportation

denverurbanism.com/2017/08/the-history-of-denvers-streetcars-and-their-routes.html

RTD (Regional Transportation District)

rtd-denver.com

Union Station

unionstationindenver.com

Art-n-Transit

rtd-denver.com/art-n-transit

Denver International Airport

en.wikipedia.org/wiki/Denver_International_Airport

flydenver.com

THEATERS, AUDITORIUMS AND AMUSEMENT PARKS

THEATERS IN THE PAST

Denverites have always enjoyed the theater and amusement parks. Enjoy a few highlights of past and present aspects of Denver entertainment.

BONFILS MEMORIAL THEATRE (ALSO KNOWN AS LOWENSTEIN THEATRE)

1475 Elizabeth St., Denver, CO 80206

It opened in 1953 as the new home to Denver Civic Theater. The theater hosted Broadway plays until it closed in 1986 and became The Tattered Cover Book Store in 2006.

coloradoencyclopedia.org/article/bonfils-memorial-theatre

CURTIS STREET

This street used to be the center for entertainment and theaters in early Denver. City Auditorium at 14th and Curtis was at one end of theater row, and the Tabor Grand Opera

House (no longer in existence) was at 16th Street and Curtis. By 1930, forty-eight theaters and ten thousand light bulbs (called The Great White Way) were on Curtis Street. But the Great Depression brought the lights down, and many of the theaters folded. Later in the 1970s, the Denver Urban Renewal Authority razed the entire street of theaters with the exception of City Auditorium.

ELITCH THEATRE AND TROCADERO BALLROOM
4655 W. 37th Pl., Denver, CO 80212

The theatre was built in 1890 by John and Mary Elitch. Mary managed the theatre after the death of John. It was the longest continuously run summer stock theatre in the US until it closed in 1987. It hosted plays, operas, vaudeville shows and music programs. Furthermore, in 1896, it hosted the first screen-projected motion picture show in Denver. The Trocadero Ballroom hosted many big bands from well-known musicians. It was torn down in 1975 due to a lack in popularity of ballroom dancing at the time. The surrounding amusement park relocated in 1995, but the theatre building still stands and is being renovated. The theatre is now a National Historic Landmark.

historicelitchtheatre.org

MANHATTAN BEACH

Denver's first amusement park (1881–1914) was also the first amusement park west of the Mississippi River when it opened. It was located in Edgewater on the shores of Sloan's Lake. In 1908, it was damaged by fire but rebuilt as Luna Park, which closed in 1914. It had a roller coaster and Ferris wheel, boat and hot air balloon rides, and a variety of animals including wrestling bears and an elephant. It had a ballroom and theater featuring opera and vaudeville.

en.wikipedia.org/wiki/Manhattan_Beach_(Denver)

TABOR GRAND OPERA HOUSE

Built by silver magnate Horace Tabor, this magnificent theater at 16th and Curtis Streets opened in 1881. Sadly, efforts to save the structure from urban renewal failed, and this beautiful landmark was torn down in 1964.

coloradoencyclopedia.org/article/tabor-grand-opera-house

CURRENT THEATERS AND AUDITORIUMS (INCLUDING MANY IN HISTORIC BUILDINGS)

Thankfully, we can still enjoy many old theaters. Some venues have changed over the years, but the buildings remain for us to use and preserve.

BLUEBIRD THEATER

3317 E. Colfax Ave., Denver, CO 80206

The theater was built in 1913. It was renamed in 1922. Currently, it is a live music hot spot.

bluebirdtheater.net

BOETTCHER CONCERT HALL

1000 14th St., Denver, CO 80202

This hall opened in 1978 and is the home of the Colorado Symphony. It is the nation's first symphony hall in the round. It is named after Colorado native and philanthropist Claude K. Boettcher.

artscomplex.com/venues/detail/boettcher-concert-hall

CITY AUDITORIUM

1385 Curtis St., Denver, CO 80204

The original Denver Municipal Auditorium was built in 1908 and hosted the 1908 Democratic National Convention. At the time of its construction, its 12,000-seat capacity was second only to Madison Square Gardens. The auditorium has gone through many transformations over time. It has had many tenants such as the Denver Nuggets basketball team and other sporting teams and events. It was large enough to have circuses and rodeos. In 1968, Led Zeppelin played their first US concert here. In 1990, part of the space was converted into Temple Hoyne Buell Theater, which is part of the Denver Performing Arts Complex. In 2005, the Ellie Caulkins Opera House, "The Ellie," honoring "Denver's First Lady of Opera" also opened in the building.

artscomplex.com/venue/detail/ellie-caulkins-opera-house

MAMMOTH GARDENS / FILLMORE AUDITORIUM

1510 N. Clarkson St., Denver, CO 80218

Opened in 1907, this auditorium has had many uses in the past and is still in operation today as a concert venue.

fillmoreauditorium.org

MAYAN THEATRE

110 Broadway, Denver, CO 80203

The Mayan opened in 1930 as a movie house. It is one of the country's three remaining theaters designed in the Art Deco Mayan Revival style. Landmark Theaters has operated it since 1986.

landmarktheatres.com/denver/mayan-theatre

OGDEN THEATRE

935 E. Colfax Ave., Denver, CO 80218

The Ogden opened in 1919 first as a movie theater, and now it is a live music venue.

ogdentheatre.com

PARAMOUNT THEATRE

1621 Glenarm Pl., Denver, CO 80202

The Paramount opened in 1930 as a silent movie house. It houses a Wurlitzer twin-console organ that was designed to accompany silent films. The organ is the largest to be installed in the Rocky Mountain region and contains more than 1,600 pipes for various sound effects. The organ, and its sister in the New York City Radio Music Hall, are the only two of their kind remaining in the United States.

paramountdenver.com

FURTHER EXPLORATION

Denver Center of Performing Arts

1101 13th St., Denver, CO 80204

Explore all the theaters in the complex and see the performance schedule.

denvercenter.org

AMUSEMENT PARKS

ELITCH GARDENS

2000 Elitch Cir., Denver, CO 80204

It opened in 1880 in the West Highland neighborhood at 38th and Tennyson Streets. John and Mary Elitch bought an apple orchard and converted it to gardens and Denver's first zoo, Elitch Zoological Gardens. Mary managed it for twenty-six years after her husband's death in 1891. In addition to the zoo, it had a theater, ballroom, botanic gardens and amusement rides. Mister Twister, a wooden roller coaster, was well-known and replicated, but tamed down in the new downtown location when the original Elitch Gardens location closed in 1994. The carousel was added in 1906 and moved to Burlington, Colorado, after Elitches closed its Highland location. The structure that housed the carousel still exists in its original location and is used for picnics. When Elitches moved downtown and reopened in 1995, it kept fifteen of its original twenty major rides. The new Elitch Gardens is located along the South Platte River in downtown Denver, but is moving in the near future.

elitchgardens.com

LAKESIDE AMUSEMENT PARK

4601 Sheridan Blvd., Denver, CO 80212

Opened in 1908, Lakeside was originally named "The White City" after Chicago's 1893 World's Fair and its Beaux Arts style. It is the only one-hundred-plus-year-old amusement park in Denver to survive into the 21st century. It has only had two owners. It used to include a swimming beach, casino, theater, dance hall and racetrack. The once-grand park, now a bit bedraggled, lives on today. The Cyclone roller coaster made of wood was added in 1940 and has been recognized as a historic coaster. The Wild Chipmunk coaster made of steel came in 1955. The carousel dates back to 1908, although it has moved a few times in the park and has added features from other carousels. The park's miniature train also dates back to 1908. Its tower, the Tower of Jewels, was one of the tallest buildings in Colorado when it was built. In its glory days, the park displayed over a hundred thousand lights.

lakesideamusementpark.com

FURTHER EXPLORATION

Amusement Parks

history.denverlibrary.org/news/
lakeside-amusement-park-celebrating-107-denver-summers

history.denverlibrary.org/gallery/lakeside-amusement-park

en.wikipedia.org/wiki/Elitch_Gardens

lostamusementparks.napha.org/articles/colorado/elitchgardens.
html

pinterest.com/guswalco/elitch-gardens

CONCLUSION

AS YOU WRAP UP READING THIS BOOK, I hope that you know more about Denver's history than you did before you began. I also hope that you are inspired to explore Denver in new ways and with new insights into its past. Maybe you will see buildings, artworks and parks with a fresh perspective. Perhaps you will become stewards of Denver's treasures in the future. I encourage you to plan excursions with family and friends and gift the book to those who might also enjoy exploring Denver.

At the time of this book's publication, we are still in the midst of the COVID-19 pandemic. As a result, some entries may not be open to the public or may not survive extended restrictions limiting their operations. Furthermore, some buildings and monuments have been damaged in protests and are fenced off from the public. I am optimistic that Denver will rebuild and restore in the coming years and will make downtown an even more treasured place to visit for residents and visitors.

I am open to feedback and may create a second edition from reader comments and suggestions and to keep up with Denver's growth and changes over time. Visit my website to communicate with me, and follow Essential Denver on social media, where you can see more photos and updates. Share your photography using the tag #EssentialDenver.

LisaJShultz.com
facebook.com/essentialdenver
instagram.com/essentialdenver
pinterest.com/lisajaneshultz/essential-denver

VISIT CHECKLIST

Enjoy this checklist for planning your next exploration.

BREWERIES

Take a tour, have a taste.

☐ **COORS BREWERY**

13th St and Ford St., Golden, CO 80401

☐ **TIVOLI BREWING COMPANY**

900 Auraria Pkwy., Suite 240, Denver, CO 80204

☐ **WYNKOOP BREWING COMPANY**

1634 18th St., Denver, CO 80202

RESTAURANTS

Ask for the house specialty.

☐ **BUCKHORN EXCHANGE**
1000 Osage St., Denver, CO 80204

☐ **CHARLIE BROWN'S BAR AND GRILL**
980 Grant St., Denver, CO 80203

☐ **MY BROTHER'S BAR**
2376 15th St., Denver, CO 80202

☐ **SAM'S NO. 3**
1500 Curtis St., Denver, CO 80202

ADDITIONAL RESTAURANTS

☐ **BASTIEN'S**
3503 E. Colfax Ave., Denver, CO 80206

☐ **BLUE BONNET**
457 S. Broadway, Denver, CO 80209

☐ **CHERRY CRICKET**
2641 E. 2nd Ave., Denver, CO 80206

☐ **GAETANO'S**
3760 Tejon St., Denver, CO 80211

☐ **LINGER EATERIES**
2030 W. 30th Ave., Denver, Colorado 80211

NEIGHBORHOOD COMMERCIAL DISTRICTS / FORMER STREETCAR COMMERCIAL STRIPS

Explore shops and restaurants.

☐ **HIGHLAND SQUARE**

☐ **SOUTH GAYLORD STREET**

☐ **OLD SOUTH PEARL STREET**

☐ **TENNYSON STREET**

CHURCHES AND PLACES OF WORSHIP

Admire the outside, view inside if possible.

☐ **CATHEDRAL BASILICA OF THE IMMACULATE CONCEPTION**
1530 Logan St., Denver, CO 80203

☐ **CENTRAL PRESBYTERIAN CHURCH**
1660 Sherman St., Denver, CO 80203

☐ **EMMANUEL SHEARITH ISRAEL CHAPEL**
1205 10th Street Plaza, Denver, CO 80204

☐ **ST. ANDREW'S EPISCOPAL CHURCH**
2015 Glenarm Pl., Denver, CO 80205

☐ **ST. JOHN'S CATHEDRAL**
1350 Washington St., Denver, CO 80203

☐ **TEMPLE EMANUEL**
51 Grape St., Denver, CO 80220

☐ **TRINITY UNITED METHODIST CHURCH**
1820 Broadway, Denver, CO 80202

☐ **ZION BAPTIST CHURCH**
933 E. 24th Ave., Denver, CO 80205

CEMETERIES
Take a walk or tour.

☐ **CROWN HILL CEMETERY**
7777 W. 29th Ave., Wheat Ridge, CO 80033
- *Tower of Memories*

☐ **FAIRMOUNT CEMETERY**

430 S. Quebec St., Denver, CO 80247

- *Ivy Chapel*
- *Millionaire's Row*
- *Mausoleum*
- *Rose Garden*

☐ **FORT LOGAN NATIONAL CEMETERY**

4400 W. Kenyon Ave., Denver, CO 80236

- *Beautifully adorned on Memorial Day.*

☐ **MT. OLIVET CEMETERY**

12801 W. 44th Ave., Wheat Ridge, CO 80033

☐ **RIVERSIDE CEMETERY**

5201 Brighton Blvd., Denver, CO 80216

STORES AND SHOPPING

☐ **LARIMER SQUARE**

1430 Larimer St., Denver, CO 80202

- *Walk this historic block.*

☐ **16TH STREET MALL**

- *Stroll the length of this pedestrian mall.*

GOVERNMENT AND LIBRARY

Each of these buildings are within walking distance from one another and next to or near Civic Center Park.

 ### BYRON WHITE US COURT HOUSE

1823 Stout St., Denver, CO 80257

- *Walk around the exterior and look inside or schedule a tour.*

 ### CENTRAL LIBRARY

10 W. 14th Ave. Pkwy., Denver, CO 80204

- *Walk around and see the outdoor sculptures and go inside if possible.*

 ### CITY AND COUNTY BUILDING

1437 Bannock St., Denver, CO 80202

- *Particularly beautiful at Christmastime when lit at night.*

COLORADO STATE CAPITOL

200 E. Colfax Ave., Denver, CO 80203

- *Schedule a tour.*
- *Stand on the steps that indicate you are exactly one mile above sea level.*

 ### DENVER MINT

320 W. Colfax Ave., Denver, CO 80204

- *Schedule a tour.*

☐ **MCNICHOLS CIVIC CENTER BUILDING**

144 W. Colfax Ave., Denver, CO 80202

- *Schedule a tour or attend an event.*

HOTELS

☐ **BROWN PALACE HOTEL**

321 17th St., Denver, CO 80202

- *Visit the lobby, particularly beautiful at Christmastime.*
- *Schedule high tea.*
- *Dine at the historic restaurants Palace Arms and Ship Tavern.*

☐ **COURTYARD BY MARRIOTT DENVER DOWNTOWN**

934 16th St. Mall, Denver, CO 80202

- *Lobby and six-story atrium.*
- *A curated collection of local art and original artifacts from Joslins Department Store.*

☐ **CRAWFORD HOTEL**

1701 Wynkoop St., Denver, CO 80202

- *Within Union Station along with a variety of amenities and decorated at Christmas.*

☐ **HOTEL MONACO**

1717 Champa St., Denver, CO 80202

- *Dine at Panzano.*

☐ **HOTEL TEATRO**

1100 14th St., Denver, CO 80202

- *Perfect for a drink at The Study or meal at The Nickel before going to the adjacent theater.*

☐ **MAGNOLIA HOTEL**

818 17th St., Denver, CO 80202

- *Dine at Harry's.*

☐ **OXFORD HOTEL**

1600 17th St., Denver, CO 80202

- *Check out the lobby and art collection.*
- *Enjoy a cocktail in the Cruise Room and dinner in the Urban Farmer.*

☐ **PATTERSON HISTORIC INN**

420 E. 11th Ave., Denver, CO 80203

- *Step inside the entry and see the hand-carved oak stairway.*

☐ **RENAISSANCE DENVER DOWNTOWN CITY CENTER**

918 17th St., Denver, CO 80202

- *Check out old bank vaults in the lounge and murals in the lobby.*

☐ **ROSSONIAN HOTEL**

2642 Welton St., Denver 80205

- *Currently not open to the public but with plans for renovation.*

LANDMARK BUILDINGS

 **BONFILS MEMORIAL THEATRE
(ALSO KNOWN AS LOWENSTEIN THEATRE)**

1475 Elizabeth St., Denver, CO 80206

- *Purchase a book in the converted Tattered Cover Book Store.*
- *Look for theater seats and other remnants of the theater.*

 DANIEL AND FISHER TOWER

1601 Arapahoe St., Denver, CO 80202

- *See the exterior and schedule a tour.*

☐ **DENVER GAS AND ELECTRIC BUILDING**

910 15th St., Denver, CO 80202

- *Visit at night to see the lights.*

☐ **DENVER TRAMWAY COMPANY POWERHOUSE**

1416 Platte St., Denver, CO 80202

- *Go inside REI to appreciate this building.*

☐ **GOVERNOR'S MANSION**

400 E. 8th Ave, Denver, CO 80203

- *Take a tour.*

 LAKESIDE AMUSEMENT PARK

4601 Sheridan Blvd., Denver, CO 80212

- *Open in the summertime only.*

NINTH STREET HISTORIC DISTRICT

Auraria Campus, Curtis to Champa Streets, Denver, CO 80204

- *Walk the street, which was converted to grass, and see the many Victorian-style homes built from 1873–1905.*

 UNION STATION

1701 Wynkoop St., Denver, CO 80202

- *Visit the lobby as well as shops and restaurants within the building.*

MUSEUMS

Schedule your visits and tours.

 AMERICAN MUSEUM OF WESTERN ART

1727 Tremont Pl., Denver, CO 80202

☐ **BLACK AMERICAN WEST MUSEUM**

3091 California St., Denver, CO 80205

☐ **CENTER FOR WOMEN'S HISTORY AT BYERS-EVANS HOUSE**

1310 Bannock St., Denver, CO 80204

☐ **CHILDREN'S MUSEUM OF DENVER**

2121 Children's Museum Dr., Denver, CO 80211

☐ **CLYFFORD STILL MUSEUM**

1250 Bannock St., Denver, CO 80204

☐ **DENVER ART MUSEUM**

100 W. 14th Ave. Pkwy., Denver, CO 80204

☐ **DENVER FIREFIGHTERS MUSEUM**

1326 Tremont Pl., Denver, CO 80204

☐ **DENVER MUSEUM OF NATURE AND SCIENCE**

2001 Colorado Blvd., Denver, CO 80205

☐ **FORNEY MUSEUM OF TRANSPORTATION**

4303 Brighton Blvd., Denver, CO 80216

☐ **FOUR MILE HISTORIC PARK**

715 S. Forest St., Denver, CO 80246

☐ **HISTORY COLORADO CENTER**

1200 N. Broadway, Denver, CO 80203

☐ **KIRKLAND MUSEUM OF FINE AND DECORATIVE ART**

1201 Bannock St., Denver, CO 80204

☐ **MIZEL MUSEUM**

400 S. Kearney St., Denver, CO 80224

- *Visit by appointment only.*

☐ **MOLLY BROWN HOUSE MUSEUM**

1340 Pennsylvania St., Denver, CO 80203

☐ **MUSEO DE LAS AMERICAS–LATIN AMERICAN ART MUSEUM**

861 Santa Fe Dr., Denver, CO 80204

☐ **MUSEUM OF CONTEMPORARY ART DENVER**

1485 Delgany St., Denver, CO 80202

☐ **WINGS OVER THE ROCKIES AIR AND SPACE MUSEUM**

7711 E. Academy Blvd., Denver, CO 80230

PARKS

Walk through and around these parks, or have a picnic.

☐ **BABI YAR MEMORIAL PARK**

10451 E. Yale Ave., Denver, CO 80231

- *Star of David*
- *Amphitheater: People's Place*
- *Grove of Remembrance*
- *Ravine*

 CENTRAL PARK

8801 Martin Luther King Jr. Blvd., Denver, CO 80238

- *Dr. Seuss-inspired playground*

☐ CHEESMAN PARK

1599 E. 8th St., Denver, CO 80206

- *Cheesman Memorial Pavilion*

☐ CITY PARK

1700 N. York St., Denver, CO 80205

- *Martin Luther King Jr. Statue and Memorial*
- *Thatcher Memorial Fountain*
- *Ferril and Duck Lakes*
- *Boathouse*
- *Summer concerts*

☐ CIVIC CENTER PARK

101 W. 14th Ave. Pkwy., Denver, CO 80202

- *Greek Amphitheatre*
- *Voorhies Memorial Seal Pond*
- *Bronco Buster*
- *On the War Trail*
- *Pioneer Fountain*

☐ CONFLUENCE PARK

2250 15th St., Denver, CO 80202

- *Dip your toes or fingers into the South Platte River and Cherry Creek.*

☐ CURTIS PARK

900 32nd St., Denver, CO 80205

DENVER BOTANIC GARDENS

1007 York St., Denver, CO 80206

- *Boettcher Memorial Tropical Conservatory*
- *Outdoor gardens*
- *Summer concerts*

 DENVER ZOO

2300 Steele St., Denver, CO 80205

- *See the many exhibits on this 80-acre campus.*

 FOUR MILE HISTORIC PARK

715 S. Forest St., Denver, CO 80246

- *Denver's oldest house*

 HIGH LINE CANAL

- *Walk or bike a segment*

Trail Map: **highlinecanal.org/guide**

☐ **OBSERVATORY PARK**

2930 E. Iliff Ave., Denver, CO 80210

- *Chamberlin Observatory*

☐ **RED ROCKS PARK AND AMPHITHEATRE**

18300 W. Alameda Pkwy., Morrison, CO 80465

- *Enjoy the views, walk the steps, attend a concert or event.*
- *Visit the Colorado Music Hall of Fame within the Trading Post.*

☐ **SLOAN'S LAKE PARK**

1700 N. Sheridan Blvd., Denver, CO 80212

- *Walk around the lake.*

☐ **WASHINGTON PARK**

S. Downing St. and E. Louisiana Ave., Denver, CO 80210

- *Paths around Smith and Grasmere Lakes*
- *Wynken, Blynken and Nod sculpture*
- *Boathouse*
- *The Field House*

ART AND CULTURE DISTRICTS

*Stroll the districts to see public art, murals, retail shops
and restaurants anytime and attend special events.*

☐ **ART DISTRICT OF SANTA FE**

First Friday Art Walk each month from 5:30–9:30 p.m.

- denversartdistrict.org/first-friday

☐ **RINO ARTS DISTRICT**

Crush Walls Festival each September

- crushwalls.org

☐ **SAKURA SQUARE**

Cherry Blossom Festival each June

- cherryblossomdenver.org

PUBLIC ART (OUTSIDE OF PARKS)

- ☐ *Articulated Wall:* Denver Design Center
- ☐ *Blue Mustang:* DIA
- ☐ *East 2 West Source Point:* Wellington E. Webb Municipal Building
- ☐ *I See What You Mean / Blue Bear:* Denver Convention Center
- ☐ *National Velvet:* Highland Pedestrian Bridge
- ☐ *Dancers:* Center for Performing Arts
- ☐ *Man and Woman:* Center for Performing Arts
- ☐ *Denver Monoliths:* Denver Art Museum
- ☐ *For Jennifer:* Denver Art Museum
- ☐ *Pilgrimage:* Denver Art Museum
- ☐ *Scottish Angus Cow and Calf:* Art Museum
- ☐ *The Big Sweep:* Denver Art Museum
- ☐ *The Yearling:* Denver Public Library

SCHOOLS
Walk around the exteriors.

☐ **EAST HIGH SCHOOL**
1600 City Park Esplanade, Denver, CO 80206

☐ **NORTH HIGH SCHOOL**
2960 Speer Blvd., Denver, CO 80211

☐ **SOUTH HIGH SCHOOL**
1700 E. Louisiana Ave., Denver, CO 80210

☐ **WEST HIGH SCHOOL**

951 Elati St., Denver, CO 80204

☐ **UNIVERSITY OF DENVER**

2199 S. University Blvd., Denver, CO 80208

- *Evans Memorial Chapel*
- *Buchtel Tower*
- *University Hall*
- *Mary Reed Hall*
- *Iliff School of Theology*
- *Art walk*

SPORTS

☐ **BALL ARENA, FORMERLY PEPSI CENTER**

1000 Chopper Cir., Denver, CO 80204

- *Attend an event or game.*

☐ **COORS FIELD**

2001 Blake St., Denver, CO 80205

- *Attend a Colorado Rockies baseball game.*

☐ **DICK'S SPORTING GOODS PARK**

6000 Victory Way, Commerce City, CO 80022

- *Attend a game or event.*

☐ **EMPOWER FIELD AT MILE HIGH**

1701 Bryant St., Denver, CO 80204

- *Attend a Broncos football game or event.*
- *Gaze up at the bucking Bronco on top of the south stands.*

 INFINITY PARK

950 S. Birch St., Glendale, CO 80246

- *Attend an event or game.*

OTHER SPORTS VENUES

 CITY PARK GOLF COURSE

3181 E. 23rd Ave., Denver, CO 80205

- *Play a round of golf.*

 DENVER ATHLETIC CLUB

1325 Glenarm Pl., Denver, CO 80204

- *Private athletic and social club; take a tour or attend*
  an event.

☐ **DENVER COUNTRY CLUB**

1700 E. 1st Ave., Denver, CO 80218

- *Private and invitation-only entry.*

☐ **DENVER TURNVEREIN**

1570 N. Clarkson St., Denver, CO 80218

- *Take a dance class and attend a dance.*

☐ **NATIONAL WESTERN STOCK SHOW**

4655 Humboldt St., Denver, CO 80216

- *Attend a rodeo and various shows and walk through exhibits and grounds each January.*

☐ **OVERLAND COUNTRY CLUB, FORMERLY DENVER COUNTRY CLUB**

1801 S. Huron St., Denver, CO 80223

- *Play a round of golf.*

THEATERS

☐ **BLUEBIRD THEATER**

3317 E. Colfax Ave., Denver, CO 80206

- *Attend a live music event.*

☐ **DENVER CENTER OF PERFORMING ARTS**

1101 13th St., Denver, CO 80204

Multiple theater venues including the three largest:

☐ **BOETTCHER CONCERT HALL**

1000 14th St., Denver, CO 80202

- *Attend the Colorado Symphony.*

☐ **ELLIE CAULKINS OPERA HOUSE, "THE ELLIE"**

1385 Curtis St., Denver, CO 80204

- *Attend an opera, ballet or other performance.*

☐ **TEMPLE HOYNE BUELL THEATRE**

1350 Curtis St., Denver, CO 80202

- *Attend a Broadway show or other performance.*

☐ **ELITCH THEATRE**

4655 W. 37th Pl., Denver, CO 80212

- *Walk the exterior only: plans for renovation.*
- *Carousel Pavilion, originally within Elitch Amusement Park.*

☐ **FILLMORE AUDITORIUM**

1510 N. Clarkson St., Denver, CO 80218

- *Attend a concert.*

☐ **MAYAN THEATRE**

110 Broadway, Denver, CO 80203

- *See a movie.*

☐ **OGDEN THEATRE**

935 E. Colfax Ave., Denver, CO 80218

- *Attend a live music event.*

☐ **PARAMOUNT THEATRE**

1621 Glenarm Pl., Denver, CO 80202

- *Attend an event.*

RECOMMENDATIONS

ORGANIZATIONS

DENVER ARCHITECTURAL FOUNDATION

Founded in 1990, this foundation looks at Denver's architectural past, present and future. The organization hosts tours, lecture series and the event Doors Open Denver each September that provides a look inside many of Denver's important and interesting structures.

denverarchitecture.org

DENVER PRESS CLUB

Founded in 1867, this club supports journalism and journalists as well as facilitates conversations about the issues of the day. It offers an annual scholarship program and other events.

denverpressclub.org

DENVER WOMAN'S PRESS CLUB

Founded in 1898, this club supports women in journalism, media, communication and literary fields. It offers an annual scholarship program, unknown writer contest, garden party, jewelry sale and educational and social events.

dwpconline.org

HIGH LINE CANAL CONSERVANCY

It was founded in 2014 to preserve, protect and enhance the High Line Canal. A guidebook, map and further information are available on the website.

highlinecanal.org

HISTORIC DENVER

This foundation was founded in 1970 as a result of many historic properties being demolished in the 1960s. The original focus was to save the Molly Brown House. Its mission was successful, and now you can tour this remarkable home and museum. The organization also offers walking tours, provides preservation resources and is dedicated to safeguarding the soul of the city.

historicdenver.org

PERIODICALS

5280: DENVER'S MILE HIGH MAGAZINE

This monthly magazine features news, adventures and culture, restaurants, health and wellness, home, family and much more.

5280.com

DENVERITE

This is a member-supported news organization for the curious and concerned in our ever-changing city.

denverite.com

THE DENVER POST

Denver's largest newspaper today, it began publication in 1892. It provides local news, sports, weather, business, politics and much more.

The Know is the *Denver Post*'s entertainment website. Discover events, music, food, the outdoors and things to do.

denverpost.com

theknow.denverpost.com

BOOKS

African Americans of Denver by La Wanna M. Larson and Ronald Jemal Stephens

A History Lover's Guide to Denver by Mark A. Barnhouse

A Short History of Denver by Stephen J. Leonard and Thomas J. Noel

Boomtown History Denver by Gayle Baker, PhD

Denver by Foot (website and books) by Chris Englert

Guide to Denver Architecture by Mary Voelz Chandler

Walking Denver by Mindy Sink

ACKNOWLEDGMENTS

Many people knowingly or unknowingly helped with this book. On the front lines of production, I first thank Ruth Letofsky who did the initial fact check and polish. I also thank La Wanna Larson for her review. Next, Jennifer Jas proofed and polished further. Victoria Wolf provided me with a cover design and interior layout.

I appreciate Tom Williamson and other staff members at the Denver Public Library who helped me gather and purchase historical photographs. I thank Moya Hansen, Collections Volunteer for the African American West Museum for her assistance and for the photo of Dr. Justine Ford. I appreciate Jeanne Abrams and Thyria Wilson for their help procuring the photo of Frances Wisebart Jacobs, courtesy of the Beck Archives, Special Collections, University of Denver Libraries. Thanks to photographer Carol Sandstead for her picture of Jerry Diaz Mexican Rodeo Extravaganza – Lisa Trujillo/Dancers:

Ballet Folklorico de Lisa Trujillo, Ballet Folklorico Sangre de Mexico Julio's dance, and Alameda High School.

Also, thanks to Polly Letofsky, guru at My Word Publishing, for her support and assistance in final optimization for the book's release.

A few friends gave me extra support and cheering during the final phase. Thanks, David Kennett, for being available to bounce ideas off of and for suggesting the word "essential." Thanks to Joseph Kerski for his help on Denver's weather and climate. His informative "Our Earth" YouTube channel is esriurl.com/ourearth. Thanks to friends Nursine Jackson and Laura Jacob, who listened to me talk about the book and championed me to completion during hikes and walks. I appreciate both my daughters' support and for Liberty's picture of me with the blue bear.

I also thank my many walking companions who hopefully enjoyed joining me on my research tours.

Note: I want to acknowledge that a city changes fast. In the last weeks before finalization of the book, the Pepsi Center became Ball Arena, and South High School changed their mascot from the Rebels to the Ravens. I did my best to make corrections until the point of finalization, and after that, I will save changes, corrections and additions for a second edition. Furthermore, at the time of publication, we were still in the midst of the COVID-19 pandemic, which meant that some establishments were temporarily closed or had limited accessibility.

ABOUT THE AUTHOR

Lisa J. Shultz is an award-winning author of multiple books. She is a member of the Denver Woman's Press Club, Historic Denver and Denver Architectural Foundation.

Learn more about her and inquire about bulk book orders at LisaJShultz.com.

As a wrap-up, enjoy a few fun facts about Lisa that show her connections with Denver:

Lisa was born in Denver, Colorado, in 1963 at St. Luke's Hospital.

St. Luke's admitted its first patient in 1881 and closed in 1992.

She worked there on-call as a physical therapist shortly before its closure.

Her high school senior ditch day took place in Washington Park and her graduation ceremony was held in City Auditorium in 1981.

She also graduated from the University of Colorado Health Sciences Center in 1985.

She studied at this medical school complex founded in the 1920s, located at 9th Ave. and Colorado Boulevard. Outgrowing its space, it was later relocated to the Anschutz Campus in Aurora in 2007.

Her first job as a physical therapist was at St. Anthony Hospital. This facility opened in 1892 adjacent to Sloan's Lake at West 16th Street and Raleigh Street.

She retired from physical therapy in the mid-1990s after the birth of her second daughter.

She began writing and publishing books in earnest in 2010.

She recently learned how to dance West Coast swing at the Denver Turnverein and has performed with a flash mob performance in front of the Daniel and Fisher Tower on the 16th Street Mall.

PHOTO AND ILLUSTRATION COPYRIGHT PERMISSIONS

Rodolfo Gonzales: call number, Z-8826

Emily Griffith: call number, RMN-026-2409

Bruce Randolph: call number, ARL-229

Chief Little Raven: call number, X-32423

Robert Speer: call number, Rh-862

Wellington Webb: call number, RMN-033-8357

The Denver Dry Goods Co.: call number MCC-1047

View of 16th St. and D&F tower: call number MCC-4234

16th Street in 1938: call number X-23375

Denver Auditorium: call number MCC-1027

Curtis Street at Dusk / Theater Row: call number Rh-77

Tabor Theater: call number: X-24744

Lakeside Amusement Park: call number MCC-3544

BLACK AMERICAN WEST MUSEUM, PAUL STEWART COLLECTION

Dr. Justina Ford

BECK ARCHIVES, SPECIAL COLLECTIONS, UNIVERSITY OF DENVER LIBRARIES

Frances Wisebart Jacob

LIBRARY OF CONGRESS

James Denver

Molly (Margaret Brown)

Federico Peña

COLORADO VIRTUAL LIBRARY

Barney Ford

CAROL SANDSTEAD, PHOTOGRAPHER

Jerry Diaz Mexican Rodeo Extravaganza—Lisa Trujillo/Dancers:

- Ballet Folklorico de Lisa Trujillo
- Ballet Folklorico Sangre de Mexico Julio's Dance
- Alameda High School

LIBERTY JOHNKE

Author photo

ADDITIONAL PHOTO SOURCES

Stock photos in the public domain

Photos by the author, Lisa J. Shultz

Made in the USA
Coppell, TX
14 March 2021